The
Opposite
of a
Person

The Opposite of a Person

Lieke Marsman

translated by Sophie Collins

This edition first published in Great Britain in 2022 by
Daunt Books Originals
83 Marylebone High Street
London W1U 4QW

1

Copyright © 2017 Uitgeverij Atlas Contact

Originally published in Dutch as *Het tegenovergestelde van een mens*
English translation copyright © 2022 Sophie Collins

'For No Clear Reason', from *Selected Poems of Robert Creeley* (University of
California Press, 1991), used with the permission of Marion Boyars Publishers

Quote from Burning Heart's 'Into the Wildness', written by
Jessika Neuman, used with the kind permission of the band

Excerpt from Joni Mitchell and Jian Ghomeshi interview, CBC Music,
04 June 2013 (https://jonimitchell.com/library/view.cfm?id=2985).

Extracts from Naomi Klein's *This Changes Everything* (Penguin: 2015)
used with the permission of the publisher

Extract from Karyna McGlynn's 'Erin with the Feathered Hair', from
I Have to Go Back to 1994 and Kill a Girl (Sarabande Books: 2009),
used with the permission of the author

A CIP catalogue record for this title is available from the British Library.

ISBN 978-1-914198-10-6

Typeset by Marsha Swan
Printed and bound by TJ Books Ltd

www.dauntbookspublishing.co.uk

ONE MORNING

this morning
is radiating
a menacing timelessness
as if to make it known
that the air hasn't changed
since 1986
as if it's possible to point
at something for more than a second
this light
seems to come from the past
as if someone back there were holding up a mirror
towards us, light
that mirror
that tries and fails to hold it
it escapes, light
because of what it means
to be a mirror
like two people
who leave each other one morning
because of what it means
to be two people
you could of course place
another mirror opposite to bring it back, light
to stop her moving away, a person
but this infinite relapse:
mirror and mirror
person and person

Staying In

1.

As a child I loved to fantasise about being a cucumber. In the evenings I would lie with my arms against my body under my dinosaur duvet, sometimes straight as a candle, other times with my legs slightly bent, and try for just a moment to take on the form of my favourite vegetable. *I'm a cucumber, a cucumber, a cucumber,* I would whisper to my eight-year-old self, until I realised that cucumbers cannot whisper. From then on I would repeat my mantra inside my head, until it occurred to me that cucumbers cannot think to themselves either. But by then I had usually fallen into a sweet, deep sleep. Nota bene: this was a time when mindfulness didn't yet exist and meditation was still something so exotic that just the idea of it was enough to send most people into a wild panic.

I lived with my parents and my brother Carl in a Vinex-wijk, a housing development on the outskirts of a medium-large town in the Dutch provinces. The houses on our street were made of white bricks held together by light grey cement. Most of the residents had painted their window frames blue, red or yellow, primary colours that appeared lurid against the pale stone. There were a lot of children living in the development and thus an imposed speed limit of thirty kilometres an hour. Family cars moved through the streets towards school and work like heavy animals, grazing bison in flatlands of straight pavements and basketball courts. Only in the evenings would you sometimes hear a car pull up fast. And every now and then a scooter.

With their holiday money the people on our street would usually buy a new parasol or a pressure washer. Or a holiday of course. Most of our neighbours would staycation like us, going camping on the North Sea coast or to a holiday park in the Veluwe, but occasionally, at the end of August, a suntanned family would ride back into the street, having pitched up for three weeks in a Spanish field with a caravan and a small marquee. They would be treated like VIPs at the neighbourhood barbecue that was held every year in the first weekend of September.

My room wasn't big, just eight square metres, but it was mine. In it was a bed, a tiny dark green dresser and an IKEA desk. Because I was in love with P, a boy from my class, I had carved his name into the desk (on the back, so that no one would ever see). When I was very small, I insisted that my room be decorated with rainbow-spotted wallpaper that made me feel as though I were surrounded by an endless stream of falling confetti. Later, pulling strips of said paper off the walls became its own bedtime ritual (along with fantasising about being a cucumber).

Trying to imagine how it is to be an object – a vegetable, a cucumber, something that grows but does not feel – is one of the most extreme tests of our empathic abilities. Mostly we understand empathy as feeling what the other feels, but to embody something that has no feelings means that you must genuinely feel *nothing*. And not in the sense of feeling momentarily relieved not to be plagued by the everyday emotions, but in the sense that to feel something – anything at all – has become an *impossibility*.

It's often said that the moment a child notices that parts of them are changing is the moment at which the child develops a sense of personal identity, but for me this same realisation occurred when I became aware that I would never really change, that I could never become anyone or anything else. This is when I first subjected myself to a critical review, because a person who cannot become anyone else must surely understand themselves as fully as possible. It might be said that this type of navel-gazing is simply an expression of narcissism, but it could equally be one of modesty; you are, after all, the only subject about which you can hope to have complete authority; to assert an objective statement about anything or anyone else in this respect is fallacious, an act of vanity.

The results of my analysis, written up in a little exercise book, read as follows:

> Ida, 8 years old
> Blonde hair
> 1 m 28.5 cm
> Will be a professor or a headteacher
> Big birthmarks on left hip and left shoulder
> One big scar on right arm (barbed wire)
> Parents: 2
> Brother: Carl, 12 years old

Hobbies: reading, drawing

Hero: Donald Duck

Favourite vegetable: cucumber

Today, meanwhile, an identical piece of research would look like this:

Ida, 29 years old

Blonde hair, first greys

1 m 76 cm

Will not be a professor or headteacher any time soon

Is, however, a climate scientist

Currently unemployed, but whatever

Large birth marks on left hip and left shoulder plus small freckles all over body

One tattoo (side of ribcage)

One large scar on right arm (barbed wire), one large scar on left knee, plus lots of smaller ones

Hobby: reading

Hero: Naomi Klein

Favourite vegetable: broccoli

2.

'Is it starting soon?' I ask.

'I don't know.'

'It should have started fifteen minutes ago.'

'Maybe someone back there fainted.'

'Or had a heart attack.'

'Wait, I think the lights are going down.'

I met the woman in the seat next to me a week ago at our mutual friend Steven's birthday. Steven is known to his friends as the guy who borrows money and never gives it back, or else who gives it back in the form of stuff you never asked for. It was while he was leading me to his bedroom to check out an antique badminton set (he owed me eighty euros at the time) that I caught my first glimpse of her. She was standing next to the kitchen door, completely alone, but not in a sad way: a small, attractive woman in dungarees, one hand on her hip. She looked me straight in the eyes. It took me a moment to notice that Steven was pulling my sleeve and shouting my name above the music.

For the rest of the evening I was painfully aware of her presence in the room. Fortunately this sense of awareness reduced in direct proportion to the amount of alcohol I consumed, so that, after an hour or two, I finally had the courage to speak to her. She introduced herself as Robin. She was thirty-two, hadn't lived in Amsterdam all that long and was working on a thesis on the Italian writer Giacomo Leopardi. After an anecdote about his doomed love life ('The love of his life turned him down because he stank!'), I asked her, with the help of a sad little story about my own terrible love life ('but as far as I know I don't stink'), out on a date.

And so now here we are, sitting next to each other in this enormous theatre whose lights have indeed just started to dim. Every now and then our legs touch. The theatrical adaptation of Michel Houellebecq's *The Elementary Particles* is about to begin. As the last of the light goes, we pretend to study the flyers we were handed at the door on the way in. Soon there will be an afternoon of East Asian film in one of the smaller theatres, I read. I take a too-big sip of beer and start coughing.

The curtain goes up and loud house music begins to play. A middle-aged man walks slowly onto the stage and shouts something to the woman following him at a distance of ten metres or so. She has the same short black hair as Robin. I blink a few times as a white spotlight appears from somewhere.

Now and then I'm able to follow the dialogue and mono-logues of the actors, but to be honest I find my thoughts drifting, especially after the break. I can't get the article I read earlier today about atomic bombs out of my head. A flash, they say. A flash, and then, if you're lucky, a crack, like thunder, but most people don't get to hear it. A few weeks ago I finished my Earth Sciences degree, and this morning I picked up my certificate from the departmental secretary. I can once again decide for myself what to become engrossed in, and, in one way or another, I appear to have chosen to become engrossed first and foremost in the subject of nuclear weapons.

The actors take their last deep bow. Robin touches my hand and asks me what I thought of the performance.

In the theatre you probably wouldn't even see the flash, though we can't be completely sure, given that the atomic flash can be up to a thousand times brighter than that given off by lightning and, who knows, one of the exit doors might have been left open a crack?

'Brilliant,' I say. 'Absolutely brilliant. I found that actor with the long hair very affecting.'

I smile at the cloakroom girl as I hand her my ticket. The code name of the aeroplane that dropped the bomb on Hiroshima was Dimples. Outside, Robin and I say goodbye to each other at our bikes. I promise her I'll call soon. She leans over and kisses me quickly on the mouth.

At home I open up Teletekst to see if there's been any 'big news'. When something's big news on Teletekst it usually occupies the whole upper half of the screen, or else the title of the piece will appear in all caps. Big news can be anything really, though if you're hearing about it for the first time via

Teletekst it probably doesn't relate to anything urgent in your immediate environment. Tonight, the most important news items are about a consultation on the national terms of employment (always at an impasse) and a fire in the centre of Zwolle. I exit Teletekst and find myself in the middle of a football cup match replay in which one of the players is being given a red card for a poorly executed tackle. His team-mates are visibly furious until, against all expectations, they go on to score the winning goal. The scoring striker takes off his shirt in a moment of wild joy, a move that will unfortunately also guarantee him a card from the referee.

Along with hunger, thirst and the desire to have sex, the undisturbed rhythm of sports broadcasts is one of the most reliable things known to humankind: whatever happens, it will continue, day after day. If, next Tuesday evening, an atomic bomb should fall on China, you can be sure that all the teams would still turn up to take part in the European Championship the following weekend, black armbands on show.

3.

I started off as a student in Political Science, and when I became preoccupied with climate change it was primarily as an engaging political–philosophical question: how to reconcile a fact like the rising of the Earth's temperature, the reversal of which requires a long-term solution, with the short-term perspective shared by almost all politicians? Even if everyone in the world were to agree simultaneously that something must be done to combat global warming, no one would put themselves forward as the first or only national government to commit to the huge expenses that inevitably come along with the attempt to heal the environment. A *real prisoner's dilemma* was the phrase that rang out at each and every lecture.

After a while, I'd had enough of all the theory. The solutions proposed on paper by political analysts sounded great, but in practice – well, in practice there was no practice at all. I asked myself what impact the metres and metres of paper produced each year by the department were having on our politicians, concluded that the answer was none and decided to transfer to a discipline I hoped would be more in touch with reality. In the last year of my bachelor's degree I signed up for a minor in Future Planet Studies followed by an intermediate year in which I caught up in Physics and Chemistry, before at last being admitted to the master's in Earth Sciences. Instead of policy I would now preoccupy myself with that which determined it: data.

At the beginning of this course I encountered Naomi Klein's *This Changes Everything* (a book that indeed changed everything for me). Research shows that the extent to which people believe in climate change is contingent on the kinds of solutions offered, writes Klein. It's for this reason that conservative liberals believe that we can influence the climate when building more nuclear power stations is what's being proposed. The idea, however, that carbon emissions can be reduced by switching to wind or sun energy only makes them more sceptical about the existence of climate change. You could therefore say that, in many instances, data determines policy, but only after policymakers have determined the data.

After our first date Robin and I begin to see each other regularly, often sleeping over at each other's places during the week. But as she becomes more and more busy with her thesis research, I have, for the first time in a long time, not much to do. I clean the house for hours out of sheer boredom. I even begin to iron my socks and underwear. Meanwhile, however, my final research project is received very enthusiastically by my thesis supervisor. The subject, the influence of shale gas mining on the quality of dykes in the north of the Netherlands, is, according to him, highly topical.

In an interview with the university magazine, I explain that there are many businesses with high CO_2 emissions that are still supported by the government – oil companies and organic industrial farms, for example. Worldwide, the fossil fuel industry is subsidised by over 5,000 *billion* dollars each year. Alongside this, many green enterprises are forced to reckon with deregulated industries that suddenly attach enormous importance to the rules when it suits them. That this is in competition with the neoliberal principle 'let the market decide', of which all of those businesses are advocates, is not something you ever hear spoken about.

Next to the interview is a large picture of my head, a photo about which my friends regularly tease me because of how seriously I am looking into the camera.

'My little intellectual,' says Robin, as she carefully cuts the pages from the magazine and pins them to her notice-board. I plan to spend the rest of my life with her, only I don't dare say so just yet.

4.

It was around the age of eleven that I first became obsessed with objects. Objects, I observed, did not say cruel things to others. That they never said anything sweet or funny either didn't really matter to me, and so I began to collect objects of all kinds: teaspoons, fountain pens, marbles, those tiny pots of UHT milk. I no longer thought about cucumbers, but I did sometimes fantasise about being a table. I didn't have to try very hard: I already felt as awkward and immobile as a heavy oak dining table, just like the one our Reformed Christian neighbours had in their front room. On Sunday mornings the entire family would gather out on the front steps. From my bedroom window I was able to study them closely. They looked so solemn with their black hats and long skirts. In their kitchen window hung white lace curtains. I tried to imagine what these people saw when they watched me walking down the street. An enormous table on wheels, I imagined, rolling slowly by. Perhaps they could see a woollen doily on me too. A doily that made my back itch.

5.

Seeing as I grew up clueless, without even a religion (though of course with a lot of rules, or at least strict parents, but no overarching principle to bind said rules together), in a city that wasn't uninteresting per se but which was exceedingly *uninterested*, I have no mother tongue as such when it comes to beliefs, no golden thread to lead me through the world. Every ideology I have come across since feels to me much like the weather: today, perhaps, very important to my chosen activity (often providing me with a reason to stay home), but tomorrow quite different. I oscillate between, on the one hand, wanting to participate more actively in society and, on the other, wanting to shut that society out completely. My compromise is to learn as much as possible about society each day. On my own, at my desk, I scan website after website, watch documentary after documentary on YouTube, visit one WikiLeaks Forum discussion after another, share images on Facebook of Donald Trump's raw chicken fillet of a head.

My thesis is held by two online databases. When I log in, I can see that no one has accessed the document for the past month (my own visits to the URL are automatically filtered out of the visitor statistics). I haven't heard anything from my supervisor for weeks. If I want to progress in this field, I will have to seek out new opportunities and experiences, make new contacts. Meanwhile, half the students from my year have accepted jobs at Shell.

I am in awe of the way Robin is able to make her ambitions a matter of public importance, as though it goes without saying that she'll be one of the most influential researchers in her chosen field within the next few years. In addition to carrying out her own research, she's a member of various action groups and committees in which she participates and delegates with remarkable ease.

6.

During one of my laps of the internet I stumble across a three-month internship at an institute in the Alps investigating the effects of climate change on the region. The project concerns the decision to remove a reservoir dam in Northern Italy, right by the Swiss border. The dam is old and supplies too little energy to justify the high maintenance costs. Additionally, dams draw on the currents from rivers, making the water warmer and its quality lower. They prevent the flow of sediment and nutrients and the migration of fish. By instinct salmon breed in the places where they were born, which makes for an impressive yearly spectacle, all those thousands of salmon hurling themselves against the mountain sides . . . until they come up against a dam, that is. We see dams as hubs of natural energy, but they raise the question of whether you can in fact use the word 'natural' when speaking of something that is essentially man-made. I read that people have attempted to maintain the number of salmon in rivers by introducing farm-raised fish. Subsequently, the wild salmon in those areas became extinct within the space of three years.

Lately I've found myself increasingly irritated at the predictability of my life. My city, my street, my apartment: all are characterised only by the fact of their not being other places in the world. Even though I hate travelling, I decide to apply for the internship. The following day I get an email back from a woman who introduces herself as my mentor. I can start mid-August.

7.

When it comes to dams, Italy is primarily known for its major disasters. The bursting of the Gleno Dam in 1923: 365 deaths. The Sella Zerbino Dam, 1935: 111 deaths. Val di Stava, 1985: 268 deaths. The unprecedented disaster of the Vajont Dam in 1963: more than 2,000 deaths. In the films of dam failures I watch I see water that looks more like dust clouds: enormous mudflows scatter in all directions, as though light as air.

The Alps, the mountains, that cluster of dark green conifers in the distance: they have for my entire life constituted the decorative background of my messy Dutch forethoughts. Every time I find myself disappointed by the nature on offer in the

Netherlands it's because I'm unconsciously comparing it with that of Austria, Germany and Switzerland. I remember the talk I gave in my last year of primary school, how I had gathered various images of rare Alpine flora to show my fidgeting classmates, experiencing anew the frustration that I felt each and every year when, at the end of May, my father would inform me that we'd once again be spending the holidays somewhere in our own country. My fascination was mainly with Germany and Austria. I adored the so-called gutbürgerliche Küche that in our home manifested once a week in the form of schnitzels and potatoes roasted in butter, the fairy tales set in the dusty German woods and, a little later, in secondary school, the sounds and shapes of the German language. That the Alps were also located partly in Italy I would not know until much later, a fact which now suits me.

The eleven-o'-clock news is showing an address given by the British prime minister. *I am always willing to compromise, but not on every issue,* he is saying. The news has a calming effect: unrest is best countered with more unrest. I sink down further and further, arms crossed over my chest, my hands clamped on my upper arms. Beneath the nearby open window, a car starts up. On the science page of the BBC website I read that you cannot dream unless you sleep for more than ten minutes. I sleep for six minutes and dream about Robin.

8.

On the night of 9 October 1963, at something to eleven, a piece of Monte Toc broke off. The enormous rock tumbled down the mountain, landing in the reservoir behind the Vajont Dam. The volume of the rock was 80 million litres, while the reservoir contained, at that moment, approximately 120 million litres of water (the Vajont Dam being one of the largest dams in Europe). The rockfall initiated a giant tidal wave that broke over the dam wall, the latter acting as a kind of ramp. Although the dam remained standing, the water washed over it, flooding like quicksilver into the nearby valley, the surrounding mountainsides ensuring that none of its gathered force was lost. The water took smaller rocks, trees and animals along with it.

On reaching the inhabited areas, it carried away buildings, cars and people.

When that amount of water moves with that amount of force, it displaces an enormous amount of air. It was said that the air displaced that night exerted more force than the shock-waves that followed the bombing of Hiroshima, blowing away the inhabitants of the nearby villages before the water could even reach them. Some came down hundreds of metres from where the air had picked them up. Some were found naked, the air having torn the clothes from their bodies. Some were never found.

9.

When I wasn't busy with my collection of objects or pictures of edelweiss, I would help my mother with the cooking. While my child's fingers removed the shells from green beans or the skins from potatoes and she occupied herself with some other, more complex task, we would discuss our day. In the background, the sounds of my father's portable radio issued from the windowsill, while he himself would be shut up in his study until supper time. A war was going on in the former Yugoslavia. Week in, week out, journalists reported the mass murders and rapes. During one such report, my mother announced that people were evil. 'Through and through,' she said, as she cleaved a carrot in two.

This statement made a big impression: if people were evil, and I wished to be good, then I had to make sure that I was the opposite of a person. In the period that followed I tried to ensure this by first of all learning to walk on my hands. Later, when I found myself unknowingly on the eve of a drawn-out, hopeless puberty, I adopted a more thorough approach by speaking as little as I possibly could, for example, even though I very much wanted to announce my opinion on everything. At other points, I would adopt an inverse approach, saying how happy I was, how wonderful things were, while I was actually in an acute state of mourning (or at least chronically grumpy) about my own existence, with pimples and other youthful afflictions galore. In my last months of primary school I tried to pass through life as a boy. During gym class I still got changed with the other girls, but I began to walk differently. Every night I would sleep with a clay penis that I had made clamped between my legs, until one morning my manhood lay in three pieces on the floor next to my bed.

10.

In one of the very first recorded stories, the Atra-Hasis, written in cuneiform on clay tablets, the god Enlil lies awake at night because the people on Earth are so loud. He sends them drought and famine in the hope that fewer people will make for less noise, but the yelling continues. Enlil is at a loss. In order to put an end to the racket he uses his godly powers to make the river Euphrates overflow. Everyone dies, except the hero Atrahasis and his family. They have built an ark and, along with a few animals, they float into the future on their thatched colossus, where, more than a thousand years later, they will become the model for the story of Noah and the Genesis flood narrative. In the Old Testament, God punishes people because they are evil, not because they're making too much noise – though you might ask yourself what the difference is.

'People aren't all bad, they can be wonderful too,' says Robin. She is worried that my reawakened interest in the climate crisis will make me bitter. 'People visit one another when they're sick, cheer each other up when they're down. When they want to surprise one another, they take each other cakes and pastries. And they're always wanting to surprise one another. People wouldn't do these things if they were evil through and through.'

11.

My parents met in the sixties, during a student protest.

'She was the only woman who dared go to the front line. And they'd sent tanks out, you know,' said my father. 'That was when I knew: that woman. That's the woman you could win a war with.' When I look at their photos from that time I see a woman who looks nothing like me. She's slimmer, more toned. Fierce. In some of the photos my father is standing next to her, a head taller, with the same straggly blond hair as me.

Now that she's retired, my mother travels the world: the Canary Islands, Thailand, a boat along the Moselle. My father, also retired, stays at home to look after the garden and the dog (Binkie). He doesn't enjoy travelling, hates it even, because he can only ever really relax in the smoking chair in his office. There's not a luxury suite or tropical beach that has anything on that chair. I rarely speak to my brother Carl and then only on the phone. He lives with his girlfriend Marjolein in the north and has a job managing a company that makes desserts. They've been trying to have kids for a couple of years but it's not happened for them yet. The last time I saw him was at Christmas. He'd brought an enormous chocolate bomb with him, into which my two youngest cousins, twins, stuck as many sparklers as possible.

12.

Robin sits on the sofa and reads the paper in a dressing gown that's far too big for her petite body. I tell her that my mother's planning to book a trip to Ibiza. '*Ibiza*,' I exclaim, 'what a cliché!' Robin says nothing. Her mother died from cancer a year and a half before we met. She finds it difficult to talk about this, and I don't dare push her.

I realise that my love cannot – will not ever – touch Robin's grief, that sometimes grief outweighs any form of love, and that's why, when we do talk about her mother, I don't stop for breath, because I don't want to allow her the space to say anything that might make me feel uncomfortable or inadequate. Sometimes I fantasise that we met each other two years earlier and that I was therefore able to offer her help and support at her mother's deathbed. It feels good for her to need me. And so sometimes I fantasise that her father dies, too, or nearly dies, and that I prepare a beautiful meal for her entire family, for all her friends and acquaintances. Then I feel good about myself. Then I feel guilty.

IF ROBIN WERE TO SPEAK ABOUT HER MOTHER:

'You often hear the next of kin say about the death of a loved one: at first I simply refused to believe it. I thought, *Marjan will just walk right back into this room at any moment. And then I'll realise that I had forgotten that she'd gone away for a week, to see her sister in London or something, as though it was me who had the brain tumour. Hi angel, she might say. I'm back! Would you grab my case out of the taxi?*

'But I don't believe that my mother is still alive, or that she'll ever come back. And yet I've been waiting for her for two years.

'And when I say I've been waiting for her for two years, I don't mean that two years have passed in which I've waited for her now and then, as though I'm waiting for her in a "global" sense, like you might wait for nice weather during a rainy spring, or the way you might briefly look forward to the beginning of the summer holiday at the end of the Christmas one. I mean I've been waiting for her in the way that you wait for an important phone call. The way you wait at the doctor's, or for a dog to bring back the stick you've just thrown. Waiting is the only activity scheduled, in other words. All day every day. Imagine it.'

13.

When Robin leaves at 8 a.m. the following morning I make the bed and clean the breakfast things. The leftover cheese rinds on the kitchen counter emit a sickly smell at room temperature. I forbid myself from going back to bed once I've finished the washing up, something I try to reinforce by putting on my shoes and splashing my face with cold water.

A few hours later I close the front door behind me and cycle to my therapist's, a journey that takes almost half an hour from Robin's. My therapist's name is Sandra and I've been seeing her for almost a year. I was referred to her by my GP after I'd attended four appointments in the space of a month with complaints about an illness that I don't appear to have.

'Are you still suffering from paranoid thoughts?' Sandra puts a coffee down for me on the low table that divides the room into two: her side, my side. The glass tabletop gleams in the sun. I first became convinced that there were hidden cameras everywhere when I developed breasts and accused my parents of filming me in the shower. I was sure that the pop stars on the posters above my bed were watching me as I undressed at night. In order to ruin the recordings, I stuck my middle finger up again and again. *Just so you all know that I know.* I now understand that the cameras exist only inside my head, but I still live with the belief that people are hatching plans behind my back to humiliate me. I tell Sandra how I sometimes have thoughts of Robin copying the key to my house so that she can have sex with someone else while I'm out, in my bed – or, a little less dramatic, that she tells me she likes me just so she can laugh at me when I say it back.

'The thing to remember,' says Sandra, as she writes something down in her notebook with a ballpoint pen, 'is that you're not as important as you think you are.'

I can't remember where, but I once read that people are rarely inclined to conceive of themselves as being one of the masses but are obviously comfortable conceiving of others that way. When someone else makes a mistake, it only adds to our perception of their mediocrity. But when you yourself fail in some way, you instantly become the worst and most miserable loser of all time. This is also an example of elevating your own importance.

I descend two flights of stairs and open the heavy oak front door of the therapy practice. It's boiling hot outside. Two tourists are eating a croque-monsieur on the terrace opposite the bike stands. A couple of leaves flutter down towards them from the tree above the tables; if they don't look out, there'll soon be birch in the Gruyère.

14.

'It's crazy that drinking never stops being fun,' I say to Robin, smiling, as we take our seats at what feels like the hundredth bar that day. My elbow lands in a puddle of beer. 'I've got a pretty well-developed mind, I think – even the best films I can only watch three, maybe four times, before they become predictable in a way that gets rid of all the fun, the excitement. But with alcohol and, I suppose, with sex, too, to a lesser degree, the excitement is always there, even when I know exactly what's coming.'

A boy in a kitsch T-shirt with wolves on it walks into the bar. He looks around and heads quickly to the furthest table at the back where a girl is sitting on her own behind a glass of white wine. She looks relieved when she sees him.

The shirt makes me think about the pack of wolves living in the deserted zone around Chernobyl. There are far more than there would be if the woods hadn't become the site of a nuclear disaster – not because the wolves are immune to the effects of radioactivity, but because it seems it's safer to live in an area where your wolf babies might be born with severe mutations than one where humans dare to tread.

'Did you know that there are action groups dedicated to reintroducing wolves into the Netherlands?' I ask Robin, pointing at the boy's T-shirt. 'I hope they manage to do it.'

15.

We have our first fight that night. Drunk, I corner anyone I can to let them know I'll be taking part in an important climate project in Italy. Robin whispers in my ear that I'm making a fool of myself. She leaves me and goes over to Wolf Boy, begins a conversation with him. Less than one minute later he's buying her a beer.

I watch them from a distance. I see him laughing hard at something Robin's said while she makes exaggerated gestures with her hands. The café is packed with people talking, dancing. The sole of my shoe is sticking to some gum on the floor. I have a sinking feeling. He is so much more handsome than I am.

I walk over to them and set my glass on the bar, hard. I pull Robin's arm and yell through the noise to ask if she's flirting with him. She looks at me, annoyed.

'Take a better look, Ida,' she says as she points at the boy who is now distracted, saying something to the bartender. 'I like women.'

I want to defend myself, but I have no case. After a big gulp of beer, I put my glass down hard, again. It falls to the floor. The two men next to us jump away from their stools, swearing.

'Sorry,' I stammer. 'I didn't mean to do that.'

'Maybe we're just too different,' sighs Robin, pushing my hand away from her arm. Before I can ask her what she's referring to exactly, she's walking towards the cloakroom.

16.

The toilet door is covered with declarations of love. Sarah and Boy, Nadja and Jennifer, Cees and Kees, María and Leroy. After a minute or ten, there's banging on the door.

'How's it going in there?'

The woman asking this question seems miles away; in reality she's not even half a metre from where I'm sitting. The floor of the stall is wet. Bits of tampon packaging float in a puddle of water near my feet. I flush and then run the tap for a few seconds to give the impression that I'm washing my hands. I open the door. When I re-enter the bar, I quickly conclude that Robin has really left.

On the night bus home I sit behind a man with a shaved head. His crown is sticking up just above the headrest, the new hair coming through looks thick. How would it feel to the touch? *It's like sandpaper*, I think, *a scalp with which you could sand the paint off a small table.*

'Yes, we are different,' I mumble, but isn't that exactly why we were drawn to each other? Because we don't want to be with someone like ourselves?

The moonlight is very bright. Huge spherical storm clouds have formed on the horizon, one in the shape of a mushroom. I imagine that the third atomic bomb has just been dropped on a suburb of Amsterdam. With every breath I take, I inhale more shame.

I try to bring to mind my loves prior to Robin. It doesn't really work. The haircuts, noses, mouths that appear before my eyes could belong to anyone. That's the strange thing about old loves: everything they meant to you becomes arbitrary, even though you're aware that you were once almost overwhelmed by the urgency and intensity of your feelings for them. For a moment, for months or even years, someone steps into the foreground, only then to step back and become subsumed into the mass, the same mass to which, from their perspective, you also belong.

THE DIFFERENCE

The difference is equal to the margin of profit: what's left over once you've subtracted what you lost from what you gained. Sometimes there is no difference between losing what you gained and gaining what you lost

The difference is that I am your mother and I can decide what time I go to bed. Now, upstairs with you, you little blade of lightning

The difference is that you might put more effort into one day than the other, which doesn't end up making any difference

The difference is a number that is not divisible by itself. If you did divide it, you'd always come out with more than one. No, less

The difference grows on trees that don't resemble one another, and in fields, at different altitudes

The difference between two people exists

The difference is dictated by time. If time did not exist, everything would immediately collapse into a black hole

The difference is that he's finished his homework and is now going to pick blackberries in the garden. You could, too, if only you'd try your best

The difference is that you work with the options that have been made available to you. Because you reject one such option, you overestimate your influence

The difference is that you'd rather do something heroic

Something to erase the difference

The difference is visible in someone else's face, when you've been looking at it all afternoon

The difference can be visualised in the form of a time lapse: two tectonic plates that split apart at speed

The difference cannot be undone

The difference makes itself known mostly during the Age of Reason

The difference is easiest to see when set against a white background

The difference is that it sometimes appears against a black background

The difference is that I took a brush and painted a different colour

The difference is that you're in the foreground

17.

Is it possible to want to speak to someone without having to speak to them? Once home, I put on the television and switch over to MTV. A somewhat round, pimply boy wants to flip his life 180 degrees for no good reason by becoming the quarterback of his high-school football team. MTV send a personal trainer after him and he's soon making great progress.

On my bedside table lies a little white book that Robin gave me, a novella by Marguerite Duras. It's been there a few days. I pick it up and begin to read. In the book, *The Malady of Death*, which totals no more than sixty pages, a nameless man repeatedly visits a similarly nameless woman whom he is paying to have sex with him. He is unable to form a genuine connection, according to the woman. He is suffering from a disease, she says, a disease which renders him incapable of love.

I put the book away and turn off both the TV and my phone.

Fact: I try to bind people to me by instilling in them a sense of guilt.

18.

'Freud would have a field day with you,' says Sandra, a few days later, when I tell her about my attack of jealousy.

'Freud is obsolete,' I say.

She walks over to the window and pushes the curtains aside to let in a breeze. On her desk is a cereal bar. She picks it up and takes a bite.

'Perhaps. But you've often shared this sort of thing. Where's it all coming from?'

'Beats me,' I say. The coffee Sandra has given me is bitter and far too strong. I expect to be wired for the rest of the day.

'Have you ever asked yourself whether you might not entirely accept, on a subconscious level, your sexual orientation?'

This makes me think of Duras. One interpretation of the book, Robin says, is as a manifestation of Duras' homophobia: the man is incapable of loving the woman because he is gay. This sounds plausible and not necessarily homophobic, were it not for the fact that Duras dubs the man diseased. According to Duras, relationships between men and women place a greater demand on the imaginative capacities than homosexual relationships do, making the former more profound. I close my eyes. Is it possible that I do not accept my sexual orientation? There's something I'm afraid of, but I don't think it's that. I would overcome my biggest fears for Robin if she were to do the same for me, but my biggest fear might in fact be that the latter will never happen. And I have to admit that I do sometimes feel ashamed of my sexuality.

'See, it's always worth examining,' continues Sandra when I fail to respond to her question. 'Think it over these next few weeks.'

When people ask me about my sexual orientation, I sometimes still answer that it's possible I could fall for a man,
maybe, who knows, and, in order to lend that statement some
weight, I tell them about my primary school boyfriend who I
was so in love with that I could no longer eat. That, during a
sleepless night full of wedding fantasies, I carved our initials
into the back of my childhood desk. Each time I find myself
repeating this story, however, I ask myself why. It's essentially
a form of lying. I'm presenting a version of myself based on
an event that, while factually true, becomes – through my
presenting it as far more significant than it really was (is) – a
kind of lie.

My one-off *infatuation* with a then-eleven-year-old boy
played itself out more than eighteen years ago, and yet I still
grasp on to it at such moments because I know that some
women will find me strange, that some men will lose all
interest in me when they realise it's never going to happen
– between me and a man, that is. I don't mean to say that,
in these scenarios, the man in question necessarily has any
sexual interest in me, simply that there is a type of invest-
ment in human relationships that is explicitly related to the
idea that you might one day come to be more than a friend
to the other person (at different moments, the same lie can

constitute a defence mechanism*). As long as you don't completely shut down the possibility of a relationship with a man, as long as you allow chance to continue to play a role ('it could happen . . .'), it's fine to date women, because all is not yet lost.

I came across one explanation for this kind of behaviour in Adrienne Rich's 'Compulsory Heterosexuality and Lesbian Existence', possibly the best-known essay on lesbianism that there is. Rich writes that it's not the case that all men (#NotAllMen) are scared of women due to Freudian reasons, but *that it is more probable that men really fear . . . that women could be indifferent to them altogether, that men could be allowed sexual and emotional – therefore economic – access to women only on women's terms, otherwise being left on the periphery of the matrix.*

The most important part of this citation is, I believe, the phrase *sexual and emotional – therefore economic.* In a capitalist society the individual who has something to sell has access to their potential consumer via the latter's needs and desires. It therefore makes sense that, in a society that is not

---

* When my driving instructor, who remarked every time we drove through an abandoned industrial park that we could do more there than just drive, would ask me if I had a boyfriend, I always said yes.

only capitalist but also heteronormative, the homosexual is the first to go overboard. To downplay or disown your homosexuality is thus to prevent yourself from being pushed to the edge of the community. Heterosexuality is the norm, not only between the sheets, but on the television, in advertisements, in business, on the streets and in politics – where, furthermore, it can also be safely said that men are the norm. To say that you are a lesbian is to shut yourself out of the heterosexual world and so too from *a man's world*.

But Rich wrote her essay in 1980, I hear you say, and a lot has happened since then. Gay bars are no longer underground by definition, TV series such as *The L Word* and *Orange Is the New Black* did pretty well, and the countless gay prides that take place annually in cities throughout the world have become major public events. To summarise, then, gays and lesbians now factor as valid consumers.

Homosexuality is, in a certain sense, easier to exploit than heterosexuality, given that a group of straight people would not recognise their sexual orientation as a credible basis on which to approach them as a unified audience. Gay people, however, can, it seems, be discussed and spoken to collectively in terms of their sexuality. I, for example, regularly visit websites designed for lesbians and obediently watch every new film or series featuring a lesbian protagonist, even if this condemns me to a low-budget Mexican soap opera or a movie about a subject in which I have very little interest – like, for example, vampires (for some reason there are a whole load of movies featuring lesbian vampires). In light of all this, it might be said that the major difference between our present situation and that of the 1970s and '80s is our success in having established ourselves as a target audience.

Identity works in part via the principles of collectivity: you seek out the collective with which you are most able to identify and adopt their concerns as your own. The downside: if that collective does not grant individual visibility to those who must necessarily form it, being a member becomes undesirable. And that is the problem as far as homosexuality is concerned: I identify with a group that is so diverse that, sexual orientation aside, I have nothing in common with 90 per cent of its members (this is also the reason that visiting your average lesbian bar is usually a disappointment: a shared sexuality is no guarantee of a good conversation). One of the greatest misconceptions about homosexuals is that they are more fearful of 'the other' than the average (straight) person, and it's for this reason that they find themselves unable to fall for someone of the opposite sex. But the person who is afraid of 'the other' will not find solace in gay society, which is considerably more heterogeneous than your average sports bar on a Saturday afternoon.

There are of course many other stereotypical images of lesbians (the femme, the butch, the motorbike-riding butch, the butch-loving femme), and so, communicated in these terms, an increase in lesbian visibility is not necessarily a positive thing. The individual who wishes to make money out of gays will most likely benefit by portraying them as a homogeneous target group. The *lack in representation* of the eighties has thus been replaced by a *lacking representation*, one that means that the term 'gay' has become the moniker under which an enormous number of disparate identities are grouped.

On the other hand, it's of course perfectly reasonable to assume that our preferences propel us towards different groups – or target audiences. Because I love sports, I'm susceptible to adverts featuring Serena Williams. Because I love reading, I go to places where I know I'll find other people who love reading. With homosexuality, however, there is something of a phenomenon going on in this regard: clearly, the fact that I love women is perceived as such an important facet of my identity that it's factored in even when the discussion is completely free of any question of love or sex. The domain of homosexuality extends far beyond its actual limits: to have lesbian sex makes you a lesbian scientist/lesbian daughter/lesbian parent/lesbian artist/lesbian prime minister/lesbian vampire.

That is strange. But am I then not a lesbian when not engaged in the act of having lesbian sex? Surely that's not the case either. It appears that the existential identity principle 'you are what you do' does not apply to sex, because if I were to have sex with a man it wouldn't determine my sexual identity. However, even if not currently having sex, the mere fact that I would like to do so with a woman does. It is interesting to consider, in view of this, that even the person who has sex just once a year will be defined by this event if it happens to involve someone of the same gender. An enormous part of our identity is therefore decided in bed: the exchanges that take place there, even if extremely infrequent, are seemingly more significant than the majority of those that occur beyond the bedroom.

'Of course it's completely fine with me if you're gay, but what I will never understand is lesbians who use dildos' – the words of my father, everyone. His statement exemplifies the belief that one's sexual orientation is strictly linked to the rejection or renunciation of the genitals of the sex to which you don't happen to be attracted. In this line of thinking, to say *I'm a lesbian* is to say also *I hate penises*, which some will further interpret as *I envy penises*. But I don't wish to renounce or declare my envy of anything, and I don't want others to believe that I do. As long as these kinds of misconceptions exist, it surely isn't all that bizarre that I'm reluctant to openly discuss my orientation. What I understand being lesbian to mean will not, I know, necessarily reflect the views of those around me, and so I'm cautious. Incidentally my father also believes that vegetarians shouldn't eat meat substitutes that resemble 'real' meat, even though it clearly isn't the shape of meat products (burgers, sausages, etc.) that most vegetarians are against, in much the same way that it's not the penis's form (vaginas and penises are an excellent fit for each other) that I reject as a lesbian. My father believes that vegetarians should have their meat substitutes served up in inoffensive blocks; should I, by the same logic, bring myself to orgasm with a Rubik's cube?

There is a fear of contagion surrounding homosexuality, as though anyone who shows the slightest interest in the topic will automatically develop gay feelings. But it is precisely that of which you have no experience that you should develop an interest in. I have always wanted, for example, to know how it feels to wake up with an erection, how it is to ejaculate or be looked at with contempt when you cry. And, just as I am often asked, *How does it feel, then, to have sex with another woman?*, I would love to read something about how it feels to have sex with a man as a woman (or indeed vice versa). Not simply in terms of a sexual act (for there is frankly too much of this kind of literature), but as an explicitly *hetero*sexual act. If being homosexual is of major importance to an individual's identity, then surely being heterosexual is too. Only, of course, we don't view it that way, because the heterosexual element of a person's identity blends perfectly into the background of the heterosexual society in which all of this plays out. An increase in the visibility of *hetero*sexuality could therefore be one way of exposing the issues that plague homosexuality.

A lot of homosexuals coming out of the closet will claim, for a while, to be bisexual (an orientation that, I wish to say here, doesn't necessarily face any less misunderstanding and/ or discrimination), a transition period in which we wade into the cold water until we are about knee-deep, hesitating there before allowing ourselves to become fully submerged, because this way we can still turn around and walk back towards the shore . . . At this point, I have to ask myself how far out into the water I have ventured. A little bit further by writing this all down, I think.

19.

'The garden's coming along nicely,' says my father, over the phone. 'Almost all of the shrubs are flowering and the grass is looking good. I've got the sprinkler on every evening.' I should really visit soon, he continues. If I'm quick, I'll be able to see the rhododendron bloom.

'I don't have time,' I lie. In reality I've not been able to plan more than a few hours ahead. I'm sleeping in later in the mornings only to walk around the house for the rest of the day with brain fog, deciding, at some point, that taking a nap is technically an activity, too, if only from a linguistic point of view. Fortunately it's almost time for me to go to Italy. I know a lot of people who've spoken about the so-called rut you get stuck in once you've finished studying, but I tell myself that

I've placed a trampoline in that rut by ensuring I've got work lined up for the coming months.

That evening I help Robin figure out the footnotes for a piece she's writing. It seems everything's OK again between us.

'I love the certainty with which Leopardi writes,' she says as she slides me an underlined passage across the kitchen table. 'A certainty that rids the doubt from my own mind.'

> In every country the universal vices and evils of men and of human society are noted as peculiar to that place. I have never been anywhere where I have not heard people say: Here the women are vain and inconstant, they read little, and they are ill-educated; here the public are curious about other people's affairs, very talkative and slanderous; here money, favour and baseness are all-powerful; here envy reigns, and friendships are scarcely sincere; and so on and so forth; as if elsewhere things were different. Men are wretched by necessity, and determined to think themselves wretched by accident.

Later we take a look at the recap of the day's tennis at Wimbledon. The competition is in full swing. After Rafael Nadal makes mincemeat of an Australian qualifier, Robin switches over to Nederland 2. A group of fifteen or so people of various ages and backgrounds are sitting in a circle. In the middle is the show's presenter, nervously glancing at the stack of index cards in his hands.

'Young people no longer have standards and values,' says an older woman to a boy of about twenty. She is standing over him, looking indignant. The programme concerns the question of whether there's a way to get more young people to the polling stations. The camera zooms in on the boy. He is wearing a too-big hat and visibly grasping for words. 'They are apathetic and cynical,' continues the woman from out of shot.

Has she ever stopped to consider the fact that such apathy might in fact be a symptom of strongly held values? I know that my apathy is the result of the state my parents' generation have left the world in, my cynicism an expression of dismay and my jokes a way of keeping going in a world that I didn't choose, that I would never choose, but a way out of which I cannot see. And the blame we place on the generation before ours is something its leaders have damn well engineered: in their carefully constructed system, opposition is eliminated as any form of dissent is framed as a luxury. Anyone who has the time to protest is not working hard enough. Anyone who is unemployed is lazy. Given a little more time, anyone who is hungry will be found guilty.

Naomi Klein in *This Changes Everything*:

> Indeed the three policy pillars of the neoliberal age –
> privatization of the public sphere, deregulation of the
> corporate sector, and the lowering of income and corpo-
> rate taxes, paid for with cuts to public spending – are each
> incompatible with many of the actions we must take to
> bring our emissions to safe levels. And together these
> pillars form an ideological wall that has blocked a serious
> response to climate change for decades.

20.

I look at Robin's back, the way her shoulders rise a little as she transfers one plate after another into the sink. Even when she's completely still everything about her seems to be moving. After she's finished washing up she disappears into the bathroom, and soon the whole house is filled with the sweet smell of shampoo. I stay seated on the sofa and put on a Joni Mitchell song. I sing along, a glass of whiskey in my hand.

The fact that so many people love Joni Mitchell (while others attempt to distinguish themselves by professing their dislike for her) because of her early folk-pop as opposed to her layered and musically interesting later albums is the subject of essayist Meghan Daum's 'The Joni Mitchell Problem'. It's the problem, says Daum, of being either judged Not Good or Good, but for the wrong reasons. As I guiltily put on a more challenging Joni song, Robin comes out of the bedroom to ask if I can turn it down a little.

Naomi Klein:

> Droughts and floods create all kinds of business opportunities besides a growing demand for men with guns. Between 2008 and 2010, at least 261 patents were filed related to growing 'climate-ready' crops – seeds supposedly able to withstand extreme weather conditions; of these patents close to 80 per cent were controlled by six agribusiness giants, including Monsanto and Syngenta.

One thing you can be certain of is that the companies currently denying the existence of climate change will be the first to offer you products to make the downfall more bearable the second we see acute effects. Want to get rich? Create a problem and make sure you've patented the solution.

Robin pauses as she's about to turn off her night light.

'Do you love me?' she asks. I think about this. I've loved a lot of different people in the past year, and I don't want to say it again unless it's going to influence the course of the rest of my life.

'Yes,' I say at last, but she's already fallen asleep – or is pretending she has. Her eyelids twitch.

I turn over and begin to count slowly to one thousand. My stomach is growling. Sometimes I find that if I think of food, I stop feeling hungry, but right now no matter what I think about – fries, pumpkin soup, Thai curry, different kinds of vegetables, cookies – it keeps rumbling. I picture Italy, placing myself in the few photos I've seen of the research institute. Next to me, Robin's breathing occasionally gives way to a soft little snore, a snore that seamlessly blends into the sound of the sputtering car I'll be driving on the mountain roads, hairpin bend after hairpin bend. I dive into a reservoir, tiny fish darting around me in all directions. I walk slowly up the driveway of the institute, the gravel making a crunching sound underfoot. I walk through the revolving doors, encountering the strong aroma of new carpet. An older woman sits behind a desk to my left. *Are you sure this is what you want?* she asks, in the voice of my mother. *If only I had a dog . . .* – the last thought that shoots through my brain before I finally fall asleep.

Naomi Klein:

> Our economy is at war with many forms of life on earth,
> including human life. What the climate needs to avoid
> collapse is a contraction in humanity's use of resources;
> what our economic model demands to avoid collapse is
> unfettered expansion. Only one of these sets of rules can
> be changed, and it's not the laws of nature.

Fun fact: the most radical capitalists claim their authority by
stating that it proceeds from an economic 'law of nature'. But
the economy is precisely one of the things that has, by definition, nothing to do with nature, let alone its laws. Imagine a
world in which time and space do not exist. And now a world
without market forces and/or real estate speculation.

21.

INTERVIEWER: You've always had a distaste for being referred to as a 'confessional' songwriter, right?

JONI MITCHELL: Yeah . . . You know, it's like, what do I confess to – I'm selfish? Mine is the most selfish generation, you know, in history. Right? What is so confessional – I'm sad? Oh jeez, you know, have you never been sad?

INTERVIEWER: You basically don't like being pigeonholed.

JONI MITCHELL: Exactly. No, I'm fluid. You know. Everything I am I'm not. And that's the way with all people if they really observe themselves.

22.

When I was ten I became obsessed with my nose. When I looked in the mirror, I would notice how my nostrils would flare, quiver, open further and further, until I seemed to have only two large black holes in the centre of my face. A pig, I thought. Others will notice this too, and they will call me a pig. And then – hup, there they'd go again. My nostrils, quivering. I couldn't understand how they could move like that. To make sure they didn't, I began to breathe only through my mouth. I avoided the mirror.

Years later, when I read *One, No One and One Hundred Thousand* by Luigi Pirandello, I was reminded again of that short-lived obsession with my nose. In the opening scene of the book, the protagonist Vitangelo Moscarda is standing in front of a mirror looking at his nose, which is hurting a bit. *Yes*, says his wife, *and what's more, it's crooked.* That observation is a shock to Moscarda. *My nose, crooked?* The damage has been done. Throughout the rest of the book his identity falls apart, or comes together, if you will, in one hundred thousand pieces.

Nothing is as easy as losing yourself. Noiselessly, it happens. Without even realising it you detach your self from yourself, dissolving into the everyday.

The Danish philosopher Søren Kierkegaard, in his book *The Sickness Unto Death*:

> The greatest hazard of all, losing one's self, can occur very quietly in the world, as if it were nothing at all. No other loss can occur so quietly; any other loss – an arm, a leg, five dollars, a wife, etc. – is sure to be noticed.

Things that people do in order to lose themselves: drink too much, train too much, eat too much, use drugs, love passionately. All of these resulting in only more loss.

FRAGMENTS FROM A FIGHT WITH ROBIN

'Talk to me, what's wrong? You've seemed so far away these last couple of weeks.'

[...]

'And when we do go out, you're drunk within half an hour.'

[...]

'I don't mean that you dislike other people, Ida, I don't think you think about them at all. You only think about yourself. You think that the key to getting along with others is somewhere inside yourself, but maybe it would help if you asked other people what they need?'

' ... '

'And thinking about yourself isn't the same thing as self-reflection, I might add.'

' ... '

'Maybe somewhere in the back of your head you're self-reflecting, but it's a self-reflection whose results will never see the light of day.'

' ... '

'Say something.'

23.

The powerlessness you feel when you hold a pen in the hand with which you usually do not write – the left hand, in my case – is comparable to the powerlessness you feel in social situations, fights most of all. You're perfectly alright, there's nothing physically out of place, but how are you supposed to proceed, how are you supposed to express yourself without shaking?

24.

Sometimes, when I'm feeling really lonely, I imagine that I'm a young hetero couple. Jan and Sara is my name, we've not known each other long, but we're inseparable. I drag myself out of bed on Saturday morning as two people, frying eggs for us both, buying bread at the organic bakery around the corner, paying an afternoon visit to the museum and afterwards – it's drizzling – on to the cinema. *Two Cokes, please.* The film is a romantic comedy or a documentary on the state of food supply chains. Jan has bought Sara an amusing keyring from the museum giftshop. At the end of the day, I return home satisfied, my belly full of popcorn, keyring clutched in my fist.

A masturbation scene that ends with the saying of the words: Don't leave.

25.

My brother's girlfriend just ended things. It seems that she doesn't in fact want children, or in any case not with Carl, who is crying to me now over the phone.

'I thought Marjolein was the one,' he says, catching his breath. 'She was so special.'

'What was special about her?' I ask. 'You're far more special.'

'Just . . . She knew exactly who she was and what she wanted. That's so attractive.'

'But she didn't want you.' Everyone desires someone who's strong in their convictions, but not so strong that they can't be brought over to your way of thinking.

I tell him that Robin has taken a week off work to come visit me in Italy and that he's welcome to come too, if he likes. He says he'll think about it, but I know he won't take up the offer. I want to say something about the argument Robin and I had, but Carl starts crying again.

'It's because of the miscarriage,' he says. 'She swears she saw an angel in the hospital. An enormous angel, white wings, the whole shebang. And I don't know what that angel must have told her, but everything's been different since then. Since then I've slept on the sofa.' I knew that Marjolein came from a Catholic family, but I didn't know that she believed in angels.

'That's awful,' I hear myself say. 'Aren't you supposed to lose your faith in times of crisis?'

I think it's just as easy to imagine someone losing their faith in times of great happiness. In happy times God is superfluous; before you know it you're forgetting why you ever wore a cross around your neck and said your Hail Marys. But when it really counts, God just has to show up. This is why we see God as the cause of bad but not of the good, the latter being something humankind credits itself with.

'She didn't think I was strong enough,' continues Carl. 'Too vulnerable for a man.' He's considering going cycling for a few weeks in the Ardennes. Chris, his best friend, has a little house out there and is also newly single.

'I know how it feels,' I say, a little later.

'What do you mean?'

'How it feels to make yourself vulnerable, but to have that offer of vulnerability left unreciprocated.'

'I've never once seen you make yourself vulnerable,' says Carl. 'For you love is all about coming out of it the winner.' He starts to breathe more heavily. 'To leave the arena with your head held high. But if it's real love you have to also be able to accept that you might be left behind with a broken neck.'

'Yes,' I say, 'and for you it's all about being left behind with a broken neck. So that you can go drink the whole summer in your friend's chalet.'

FOR THOSE WHO ARE SAD

For those who are sad, everything feels far away: your friends' houses, the supermarket around the corner, the work you managed to do yesterday, the toilet you just paid a visit to – even the bed you've been lying in for days doesn't necessarily feel all that close.

Of course, you can lie in bed for days without feeling terrible. Practically speaking it's a good place to be: warm, soft and usually within arm's reach of a stack of books. Tired is not the same as sad, inertia not always a sign of boredom.

In the past depression was often described via the term 'Weltschmerz': an unfulfillable longing for more or less everything in a world that always came up short and could never fully satisfy the demands of the spirit. Thus: world weariness. But in the twenty-first century, Western depression is mainly characterised by a lack of desire due to a lack of lack, i.e. due to abundance. The roles are therefore reversed: the spirit can never live up to the demands imposed on it by the modern world, a world that constantly imposes itself in the form of sounds, images, notifications, opinions. Longing no longer exists if every longing is immediately resolved, because a longing that doesn't last at least for a while cannot be called longing.

The result is strange enough: days of emptiness. Days that flow into one another bearing an apathetic form of grief, however paradoxical that might sound. The everyday contains within it a sense of not being able to continue, of feet stuck in the cement of your disimpassioned mind. Whatever you do, you feel nothing. Whatever you feel, you do nothing. An endless horizon, which nonetheless appears as a dead end.

Things that can evoke apathetic grief:

    a camping outlet on the top floor of a warehouse
    a car showroom on a Tuesday morning
    the smell of a leather sofa in somebody else's home
    their cold tile floor
    their air freshener
    a bargain footwear shop from the nineties
    advertisements
    magazines on a glass waiting-room table
    a planter full of clay pebbles
    and, needless to say, a near-deserted airport, well
       after midnight

26.

One morning, when I was nine, I found two small round balls in my bed, whiteish yellow, a little under half a centimetre in diameter. I was convinced that I had got my period. I knew periods had something to do with making eggs, and these were, unmistakeably, two little eggs. Where could these balls have come from except me? But it was far too early for me to get my period, I'd be the first in my class. My social life would be over. No girl wants to be the first in her class to get her period (a desire for which there is no clear reason, just a kind of instinct). Still I kept the eggs safe in the Chinese jewellery box in which I also kept my milk teeth. After a few days I decided to forget about the balls. Maybe I'd been mistaken about my period. Getting your period was supposed to hurt, I had heard, and I had not felt any pain. But precisely one month later there were two new minuscule eggs in my bed, and so my theory about my period was confirmed. I didn't dare tell anyone, but I knew that everyone could see it on me. Perhaps even smell it. I tried to trick my parents into thinking I was sick, but because I didn't have a fever, they sent me off to school. To reduce the chance of being unmasked I secretly placed a sanitary pad of my mother's in my underwear. During the day, however, no eggs appeared.

It was a few tough weeks, up until I discovered that one of my favourite stuffed toys, a small dog, had a little hole in his belly. A hole out of which small white balls would now and then emerge. It wasn't me but Waffie that was laying eggs. Not for another four years would I have to think about my period. When it finally happened, I was among the last in my class. Something which also gave me plenty to worry about.

27.

It's my last evening in Amsterdam. I've tried to fit as many sheets of pasta into an oven dish as possible, placing layer after layer of finely chopped vegetables and lasagne on top of one another, like a human 3D printer.

'Did you know that people are so intelligent because one of our ancestors discovered that you can cook food?' Robin says as she places the piping hot dish on the table. 'The intestines have less trouble digesting it cooked. And so the excess energy could then reach the brain, which over centuries and centuries began to grow.'

I burn my tongue on a bit of tomato and curse the ancestor in question.

After dinner we stand on the balcony and look out over the city. Even though I can't see through the houses, I assume everyone is celebrating summer. The sound of people laughing in the park on the corner carries on the smoke of their disposable barbecues. Robin picks dried flowers out of one of my flowerpots, their straw-like stems crumbling in her hands.

'Tonight feels like the beginning of a long vacation,' I say. 'Not like the beginning of three months of hard work.' It's a feeling that is reinforced by the email I received that morning: I had been looking forward to staying in a stately old Italian house, or at least a cosy apartment with a balcony and pastel-coloured walls, but the director of the research institute sent me the address of a holiday park where they've booked me a cabin.

Because Robin has an important presentation early the following morning, she heads home, and I see out the rest of my last evening in the Netherlands alone. I drink another glass of wine. I know I want to leave, and I also know that I want to stay.

28.

Very few people believe in the existence of the soul and yet we hold on to the idea that every person has a single essence. This ingrained notion that everyone has a single, self-identical consciousness creates an expectation that said consciousness is consistent and logical, which in turn makes it impossible to attribute to one person contradictory characteristics. And yet we all regularly experience conflicting feelings. You can be fearful and brave at the same time (in truth, someone who isn't fearful can't by definition be brave), and you can want to leave a place and want to stay there, too.

Aristotle's law of non-contradiction states that contradictory propositions cannot both be true in the same sense at the same time, that someone cannot both say that a thing is something and that it is not something (*p is the case / p is not the case*).

Aristotle was wrong. Someone can in fact say this, very easily.

The French mathematician and philosopher Blaise Pascal:

> This twofold nature of man is so evident that some have thought that we had two souls. A single subject seemed to them incapable of such sudden variations from unmeasured presumption to a dreadful dejection of heart.

Not until half three in the morning do I crawl back under the duvet (even when it's warm outside I like to sleep under thick bedding; my limbs need something heavy over them to allow them to feel like my limbs). Robin is kilometres away and has probably been asleep for hours. Our first date now feels like it was years ago. I set three alarms so that I can be sure I won't miss my flight later that morning.

29.

A common misconception about depression in teenagers is that they are indifferent to the world, that nothing matters to them. Everything matters: depression can just as well arise out of an excessive desire for life as from a lack of impetus. I wanted to change the world, but my world was the tiny housing development that I walked across every day while going to and from school. Schools are designed in such a way that students are so bored they can only be forced to work under threat of detention or bad marks. But the opposite is just as true: that the fourteen-year-old's desire for life is so strong that nothing can satisfy it, which can make that teenager feel incredibly depressed.

However much I loved my fountainpens, teaspoons, shells and unusual stones, I felt, at a certain point, that I needed more. And so I began to collect books. If you close your eyes occasionally while reading a book, it can feel as though you're having a conversation with the author. I brought anything and everything I could find back to my room: children's books, novels, poetry collections, art books, catalogues, biographies, textbooks . . .

When I thought about writers, I saw before me people who slowly, and with all the time in the world, put one word after the other on paper in a poorly lit room, crossing something out now and then, only to begin again, tearing a page, but gently, knowing, trusting, that the next would bring more luck.

I read more and more. My new friends were funny, clever and available twenty-four hours a day. They lay piled up in a high wall around my bed. My preference was for books written by women. Sad, strong women. I wanted to be like them, women with vibrant social lives but who needed no one. I was exactly the opposite: I had no social life and yet needed everyone.

I HATE THE STORM, I LOVE THE STORM

people who are afraid of death vs people who are afraid that life may simply continue after death

the irrepressible knowledge that you can only be in one place at one time. and the victorious feeling that follows: no one can take your place for you

descriptive, prescriptive, creative, destructive, reflective (as a sequence of analysis): describe what is, identify what should be, what should be made, what should be destroyed, reflect on what was

getting old like watching the freezer defrost: you know what you're waiting for but it feels like it's taking forever

dropping someone off at a dangerous junction and looking back in the rear-view mirror to see that that someone was you being so involved with your phone on a given day that your own thoughts become inaccessible to you. it makes you want to give yourself a call

crossing the street without taking anything at face value: every building becomes a series of lines, every tree an illustration of a type of tree, every person an archetype

discussing old loves with a new love in such a way as to say: maybe you're not quite there yet but this, this and this person really did love me (in other words: it is possible to love me)

taking it personally when things break, getting mad when things don't work out as planned

the feeling of shame like a fountain whose water keeps streaming, your heart its tiny pump

fear as both a socialising and an individualising force: you'd like to see more of others, which means seeing more of yourself – as the basis, the starting point riddle: a juggler who's left with nothing but blood-covered hands. what did he throw in the air?

on tuesday and thursday afternoons the cars outside sound different, duller

a person is to an angel what an animal is to a person

flipping through the atlas to get your imagination going

the stench of anaesthetic

laughing hard and long to drown out the storm

The Great Outdoors

Into the wilderness, away from the loneliness

— Burning Hearts

HOLIDAY ACTIVITY BOOK (EXTREME HEAT EDITION)

Quiz:

You're going travelling
a) to see more of the world
b) to escape your own world
c) to show the world you're someone who travels

Make up a holiday metaphor with reference to social skills that is better than the given example.

The given example:

When someone says something nice to you, it's as though they're throwing you a life ring.
When you say something nice to yourself, it's as though you're swimming against the current.

Stick a picture of yourself in your swimming things here, a picture in which you feel you look your best.

Stick a picture of your love in their swimming things here, a picture which shows them exactly as they are.

A problem: it's so hot that you can't bring yourself to eat anything. Solution: make sure your food is fragrant. Did you know that during summer smells spread more easily because higher temperatures increase the space between molecules?

Make up some more nonsense-facts like the above.

Play the following game: who will be the first to see a seagull poo mid-flight.

Klaverjas, chequers, Triominoes, travel Monopoly, I spy, tag, gin.

Stay inside or go in search of the coolness of dense foliage. In instances in which you encounter a pine forest, there are always cool spots to be found. And even a bare hill will have a shady side.

Find a poem with the word summer in its first line. I'll start:

> In summer, I remember where I'm from and why
> my knees smell like yellow onions –
> why you, Erin, are standing in my living room
> straddling your brother's outgrown Huffy –
> you want me back in the cul-de-sac badlands.*

Put the fridge on the lowest setting.

And the freezer.

And those of your neighbours (bonus points).

Wait until night falls.

Get moving.

Walk slowly out of the street (out of the campsite/holiday park/into the woods/in the direction of grassland).

Come to a stop in front of the first body of water that you encounter.

If it hasn't rained in a long time, there will be a shallow ford.

---

* From 'Erin with the Feathered Hair' by Karyna McGlynn

1.

It's busy at the station from which my bus is about to depart. A woman wipes a blob of jam from her son's cheek and yells something in his ear I can't understand. My jumper is dark with sweat at the armpits.

There are a lot of people on the street, each and every one of whom has a flushed head due to the scorching heat. They are dragging groceries or children, or pushing carts. The landscape becomes dustier as the bus moves further away from the airport, the city. Gradually the number of residential houses decreases and the number of wholesalers and retail parks increase. On the edges of the motorway, new and second-hand cars and cranes flash in the sun. The barriers on either side of the road are deep red with rust. The bus takes an exit towards the north, in the direction of the Swiss border and hills that later become mountains (at what point does a hill become a mountain?). Every now and then people step in or out of the bus. I help an older woman place her bags in the luggage rack overhead.

While the bus travels from one valley to another, I alternate between looking outside and rereading Marguerite Duras. I imagine the room with the sea view in which the man and woman meet: white, with only a bed and a chair, salt embedded in every fibre.

Sea. Sea. Sea. Sea. Sea. With my eyes closed, the bus's negotiation of the poorly maintained roads feels like being carried by waves.

Robin adores the sea. That gigantic, pulsing body of water, that endless plain beneath which God knows what is going on – for her they're symbols of possibility, of freedom. I, on the other hand, have hated the sea for as long as I can remember. Of course, the sea at sunset is beautiful. A tropical island is beautiful. But beach and sea are above all places where there is nowhere to hide. Where the wind has free rein. Where, three years after you drown, your bones might be found among plastic bags and driftwood by a class of beachcombing school children.

It's almost one o'clock. Robin is probably making moves to go somewhere for lunch. I picture her seated at the café she likes to go to, at the centre of the conversation, her colleagues laughing at every one of her jokes. She is ordering the tomato and pesto sandwich and is wearing her light blue slip dress, which is her favourite piece of clothing at this time of year because of the way the colour complements her tanned shoulders.

The air conditioning in the bus buzzes loudly, a strange mechanical noise that, after a while, appears to be coming from inside my own head. In the background is the murmuring of cars zooming past. I put my headphones on.

2.

What would remain of Robin and me if I no longer put her on a pedestal? I feel something for someone, and, yep, there we go – there they are, on a plinth made of white marble. Suddenly, everything they say is full of meaning, even if they say something dumb or nonsensical or send emails full of spelling errors. I bend myself into the strangest mental positions in order to find the positive in incoherence. But do you know what is even more stupid? *I am the pedestal.* To place someone on a pedestal is to say: that person is above me, but they are still within arm's reach (without a pedestal, no statue; without me, no you). What I do is attribute to that person all of my knowledge, all of the things that will enable them to understand me more fully. I want to show that person everything I see, and then worship this idealised being for that which does separate us: the fact that they are not me.

In this way I completely ignore the fact that this someone else is able to comprehend so much more than me, or to see more, anyway, but only because in my state of idealising lovesickness I haven't left the house in days. Because it turns out that without me, there is a you.

MOUNTAIN DWELLERS SPEAK OUT

Everyone is obsessed with the sea these days. Well, they can have it, just keep it away from us up here in the mountains. Because up here the sea is no use to us. Bring the sea to the mountains and we'd flee to the highest peaks, just as when a city floods and its citizens take to the rooftops. But – what would remain of our peaks? The deepest point of the deepest ocean – the Pacific Ocean – is more than eleven kilometres deep, while Mount Everest, our highest mountain, is only 8,848 metres high.

The danger of the sea is that it can appear on the surface as though nothing is the matter – but beneath, beneath is a different story. A mountain, however, shows you everything: here it all is, here are the pine trees with the deer roaming between them, look no further.

Illustrative proverbs:

If the sea is in the man, the man's gone overboard.
The beach umbrella may be in the car, but you've still got
to round up the children.

She who runs away with the sea leaves behind an ocean of dead fish.

Duras, in *The Malady of Death*:

She asks if you've seen the sea, asks if it's day, if it's light.
You say the sun's rising, but that at this time of year it takes
a long time to light up the whole sky.
She asks you what colour the sea is.
You say: Black.

You cannot see the sea behind the mountains, but you can see the mountains behind the sea. There, the sea is not out of place. But does anyone ever consider the underwater mountains? Who climbs them? Who paints and draws them? This is the fault of the sea.

Symptoms of seasickness: dizziness, nausea, puking, headaches. Symptoms of altitude sickness: dizziness, insomnia, loss of coordination, loss of consciousness. I'd rather be seasick, you might think. We think: there's not that much difference. You can drown or you can fall into a chasm. You can lose someone in the blink of an eye.

In any case, there's no middle ground. It would be ridiculous if there were people who lived on flat land, in a landscape that stretched out forever like the sea but without the sea's ability to fulfil that promise. They say: A low horizon fixes one's thoughts to heaven. We say: Heaven is empty.

We say: Black.

3.

I can remember the last time I was at a holiday park very clearly. My mother had an allergic reaction to the water from the stream next to our cabin. Carl and I slept in a bunk bed for the first and final time. He was in the top bunk and would fart on purpose before going to sleep each night. To get my revenge, I would push my feet into his back every time I suspected he had fallen asleep, right up until the moment I would doze off myself.

Here it does not smell of farts but of pine, a pine forest of the spacious, friendly kind – not the kind that becomes pitch black and impenetrable within metres of entry, where wolves reign. Twilight Forests, I used to call those, because it never seemed to be day inside them.

After a brief quest, I locate my new home, light pink with a small sign reading '103' next to the front door. Each of the little cabins is painted in a different colour and does not appear to be much more than five years old. Concrete and glass. Here and there holidaymakers sit on the stone porches in front of their cabins, wine glasses and dishes of olives on the plastic tables in front of them. I drag my suitcase into my own cabin and let Robin know that I've arrived safely. That evening I watch an Italian quiz show. I understand very little. I go to bed early: I've got to pick up my hire car at nine the following morning.

4.

The director of the research institute greets me in the hallway of a big round building with three floors. He is a tall, handsome man in his late fifties wearing a grey suit covered in dust. I've parked my hired Fiat directly outside the entrance following a stressful journey.

'As you know, we conduct all kinds of research here,' he tells me during our brief tour. 'You could say that we're the most important research institute this side of the Alps.' He leads me down long hallways with dropped ceilings. The place smells of soup.

'One of our concerns, for instance, is deforestation, both independent of and in relation to the winter sports industry. Also, in terms of global warming, the influence of meltwater on the water quality elsewhere in the country – and on the wellbeing of the animals living in the surrounding environment, of course. We're working closely with Switzerland, France, Austria and Slovenia.' We enter a large, round space. 'This is the visitors' centre. Each quarter we present our latest findings here.' He pushes a button and the strip lights come on. At the far end, to our left, is a large-scale model of the dam and reservoir. The director shows me how the sediment they've gathered and deposited behind the dam is putting enormous pressure on the dam wall.

At the end of the morning the director sends me on to my internship mentor. Her name is Chiara. She is dressed completely in black and wears thick, black eyeliner. I guess she's roughly ten years older than me. Chiara offers me a cup of watery coffee and then leads me to the workroom, which it appears we'll be sharing. The view is pretty dull: two concrete buildings – one an office, one a storage space. But just beyond you can see the mountains, or at least a small piece of *a* mountain.

'The warmer the Earth, the less snowfall,' she says during our first lunchbreak together. She's placed two sandwiches on a plastic tray. We're in a small canteen. There's a large pot of minestrone on a hotplate. 'And when the snow that would normally fall in the autumn begins to be replaced by rain, water levels will rise during those periods. The rain has arrived earlier and earlier these past couple of years, and this will only increase in severity. The dam is old and cannot handle that much water, certainly not in combination with a growing amount of sediment. It may suddenly become dangerous. Worst case scenario, we'll need to evacuate eighty-thousand people.' I bring a spoon of soup to my mouth and look past her, outside. It's raining.

'You knew all this, right?'

I didn't know anything about the consequences of snow giving way to rain.

'It rarely snows in the Netherlands,' I say, even though that's no answer at all.

snow

we're listening to the crackling of the fire

that the silence of the night behind the fire allows us to hear it's a fire that would keep wild animals at bay

were it not for the walls doing that already

in this way

the crackling of the fire sets me thinking

I imagine a long procession of animals walking towards me

when it snows

the silence of wild animals becomes even more silent

and you can see where they've been walking

but let's be honest, it rarely snows here

the pure noise erases any prints

5.

The work is simpler than I first thought: instead of conducting my own research, I'm to incorporate the results from Chiara's research group into a report for the European Union. In addition, my task is to convince as many journalists as possible to write about the project and to make sure that a good film crew is in place for the moment of the dam's demolition.

'The problem is,' says Chiara, 'that if a thousand people were lost to a bomb explosion somewhere, we'd hear about nothing else for weeks. But every year a flood or drought will take place somewhere that costs at least as many lives, and the only glimpse you get of it – if you do get a glimpse of it – is a tiny mention at the end of the news report. Most deaths resulting from global warming aren't even attached to natural disasters like these; they take place more gradually, one by one, mostly due to so-called "natural causes". As, for example, when a harvest fails somewhere, which causes a riot to break out, during which someone gets trampled; or perhaps because somewhere a road has been submerged, and someone is unable to get their medication in time. They do not send journalists to report those sorts of deaths, and so global warming features far less in the news than it should. When fault cannot be wholly or fully attributed to one source, we are less interested in disaster. But that does not mean that the fault does not exist.'

'We're going under thanks to our own successes,' she says a little later. She's just placed a pile of papers on my desk and is now returning to her own chair. 'We've become so good at rehabilitating sick kids, adults, old people – everyone, in fact – that the world population just keeps growing. One of the main goals of modern science is to make cancer a chronic illness. Well, as long as there's no substantial decrease in the number of children coming into the world, I can't bring myself to consider this. We must choose: either we keep on producing as many children as we are now and accept some premature deaths in line with the survival-of-the-fittest principle, or we try to make each living person's life as long and enjoyable as possible but ensure that the world population is drastically reduced. Luckily, things seem to be heading in the right direction here in Italy, but the same can't be said for the rest of the world.'

She opens her desk drawer and takes out a book. *The World Without Us* is the title on the cover. Before I can say anything she's stuffing it into my bag. She then stuffs some papers into her own backpack and leaves for a meeting.

On my way back to the holiday park I replay my first workday. At the entrance I encounter two boys of about eleven dragging a plastic crocodile behind them. They disappear into one of the cabins.

How many of the people I love would have reached their current ages two hundred years ago? Most would have already died of diseases they have presently survived – or have never contracted. It's impossible to say which of us would, without the DTP vaccine, have died of polio or diphtheria. Friends and acquaintances who were born prematurely, anyone born with pernicious anaemia or following a complicated delivery, anyone ever saved by an ambulance and its defibrillator, by chemotherapy or AIDS inhibitors – they'd all be long dead.

As I drive further into the park I message Robin to tell her I love her and miss her, and I almost crash into a tree. Every now and then I see a flash of lightning beyond the mountains, followed by thunder that ricochets off the mountain slopes, making it seem to come from all sides at once. I think for a moment about my atomic bomb obsession from earlier this year. I quickly park the car and hurry inside through the now-dark day.

6.

That tackling global warming begins with having fewer children is something that is frequently met with a lot of resistance. Almost all the comments on a related website I visit that evening contain at least one mention of the word 'ecofascist'. Striking is the way in which the commenters glorify the child as sacrosanct by definition, a perspective that is manifest in the use of the phrase *leave the children out of this!* But the experience of having been a child is in fact the one thing that each and every living adult has in common – which means, of course, that childhood and the child itself are less than unusual. Above all, there are, and let's be honest now, pleasant and not-so-pleasant children. But whatever they do, we see their acts as pure and, even less credible, free of worldly worries, of anxieties.

I think we've simply forgotten the kinds of admittedly trivial thoughts we were plagued by as children. Whether we would make friends on our first day of school. Whether or not we had got enough Kinderpostzegels, the little stamps we bought and sold each year to raise money for children's charities. Whether or not our birthday was near. Maybe there are children who had no such nagging thoughts, but I would wager that those children became the kind of people who, in later life, could shake their adult worries off with relative ease. Carefree people were as children no different than they are now: the child ought not to be characterised by a supposedly inherent lack of neurosis. We would like to detach the child that we once were from our adult selves in order to avoid acknowledging just how much of our personality was already present in childhood. Maybe you think it's life that made you unhappy – or love, specifically. But remember, you were always a nervous wreck.

7.

That night, before I go to sleep, I read the first chapter of *The World Without Us*. It turns out to be a book about the lasting influence of humanity on the world around us. In the book, the author Alan Weisman imagines a world in which, from one day to the next, the entire human race disappears: what would remain? How long before all trace of humankind would be erased? And how do we make sure that humankind doesn't destroy itself by destroying the world? Weisman's answer: have fewer children. If all women were from now on only to have one child, the world population would be halved by 2075.

Still, if Robin were to ask me, I'd immediately want to have a child with her. Just the thought of it makes me happy. But you can throw away with that idea any notion of contributing to a better environment. I try to summon Robin's face and body, but I'm unable to establish a clear picture. Of the last few months I can recall only snippets, mainly snippets of our arguments.

They say that depressive people have a disrupted sense of time, that, for them, time barely exists. This is because the function that time usually serves is lost. Past, present and future no longer have meaning. For the non-depressive person, time ensures that bad experiences pass, that hope is possible, that you can look back with full nostalgia on a carefree summer . . . But the depressed person can no longer properly experience the opportunity for change that the passing of time can bring. In depression, all experiences cease. There is just one experience left: that of non-experience, a long, sickly sludge of monotony. As a consequence of this, it becomes difficult to make decisions, because in order to do so you have to have a certain amount of foresight: what kinds of advantages and disadvantages will that decision afford you in the future? Some people describe depression in terms of time standing still: they acknowledge that while for the rest of the world time continues to function as normal, it feels as though they themselves have been shut out of it. The ultimate experience of 'living in the moment', you could say. And also the reason I hate to live in the moment.

That night I dream that I am the last person alive on Earth. How long would it take for me to realise that something was amiss? And how long until I would give up trying to find other people?

When I wake up the following morning I find myself thinking about the film *Home Alone*.

8.

what our wasted imaginations present us with when we think
about time stopping: a clock with an empty battery

9.

Chiara bombards me with numbers that show that the Netherlands will be one of the first countries to encounter major issues as the sea levels continue to rise. I get the feeling she's blaming me for the negligence of the Dutch government. I wish I had more information to hand on the Italian situation. She sketches an awful scenario in which dykes don't collapse but simply overflow.

'The Netherlands and Florida,' she says. '*Mark my words*. Those are the places that will open the eyes of the Western world.' She follows this with an anecdote about the mayor of Miami who elevated the entire city in the hope of buying some extra time. Postponement of the inevitable, according to Chiara.

Sometimes I can't rid myself of the impression that hope and fear, however much they are figured as opposing emotions, are in fact expressions of the same feeling: they are both a form of anticipation of the future. In the first instance, that anticipation is negative (everything will go wrong), in the second positive (everything will come good). Where I maintain hope in a good outcome, Chiara's hope has turned to fear (and the fear, it sometimes seems, into resignation).

I lay out this thought in an email to Robin after lunch, and she responds within the hour: *I don't see how hope and fear have the same characteristics except that they're both irrational – and all emotions are irrational.*

Clearly.

Is it possible to hope for something without becoming scared that the thing you hope for will never materialise? Can you convert the fear that you will suffer loss in your future into a hope that this will not happen? In any case, I know that I have never felt as hopeful as during those periods in which I was being most tested by fear. *The two therefore go hand in hand*, I write back. After I've clicked send, Chiara suggests that tomorrow we visit the reservoir with Stephan, a colleague from the animal welfare department.

10.

The strange thing about fear is that the world is just the same as it was before the fear set in, and yet everything appears changed – precisely because it feels as though nothing will ever change. How can I explain? It's as though the sky is moving before your eyes: you see what is there, but you're seeing it through a thick haze. Imagine the warmest possible summer's day, the asphalt shimmers and steams, and you are lying with one cheek on a sweaty slab of tar and stone having suddenly understood that everything you see is an illusion. How can I explain . . .

Fear: as though you, measure of your own world, have suddenly been pulled out of said world, and yet every fibre of you is still present within it, trapped within that which previously existed beyond your self. It's not you experiencing the fear, but rather the fear observing you as though from a tower, a panopticon. Or vice versa: it's as though the entire, colossal outside world has suddenly penetrated every one of your cells, taking control of your body, and yet it leaves you with ultimate responsibility. Or: fear as something which cannot access your core, but which understands how to surround that core, to brick it in. Bathe it in that wretched yellow light.

11.

Jean Rhys on hope in *Voyage in the Dark*:

> The clothes of most of the women who passed were like caricatures of the clothes in the shop windows, but when they stopped to look you saw that their eyes were fixed on the future. 'If I could buy this, then of course I'd be quite different.' Keep hope alive and you can do anything, and that's the way the world goes round, that's the way they keep the world rolling. So much hope for each person. And damned cleverly done too. But what happens if you don't hope any more, if your back is broken? What happens then?

It's funny how hope is something we expect to be doled out for free, something that simply exists no matter what – if not here and now, then just around the next corner, while of course we know, living in a capitalist society, that hope is something that comes at a price, just like everything else. Of course, there is always the negligible chance of a miracle, which one will inevitably hope for, but there's no question that not everyone is afforded an equal store of hope. You have to chase it, to do something in order to attain it. You have to save for a house. Or become pregnant. Or perhaps take up an internship.

12.

The only things to suggest that other people visit this place every now and then are the asphalt on which we're driving and the traffic signs warning against the possibility of rockslides. Stephan, a surly-looking Swiss man of about fifty whose research at the institute is focused on freshwater fish, drives quickly and recklessly – one badly judged turn and we'd sail through the roadside barriers. Two birds of prey are circling in front of us. One dives suddenly down and out of sight.

After one last hairpin bend, the reservoir and its dam finally come into view. This is what it's all been about: an enormous, broad wall with a gentle curve, grey and angular despite its semicircle shape. A drizzly Thursday morning like this is not when tourists tend to visit the structure. The view is somewhat uninspiring. The water in the reservoir is far less blue than it appeared in the photos, probably because the sky is currently grey.

Apart from the sputtering of our boat's outboard motor it is silent on the water. The light mist and mountains form a soundproof wall around the artificial lake. Its banks are deserted. In some spots the water meets a steep rockface, at others it flows onto small strips of pebble beach. Temporary waterfalls have formed along the rock faces thanks to the rain. I look again at the dam, which is now directly in front of us. From this side, the dam sticks out just ten metres or so above the water. I imagine how this massive structure, this enormous block of concrete, will, in just a few weeks' time, be wiped away by a series of short, successive blasts.

Stephan tells me they don't really know what will happen to the leftover land once the reservoir is gone. It's remarkable, he thinks, how deconstruction is largely understood as a means of tearing something down simply in order to build something new. Whoever wants to deal with ancient values or traditions must first come up with a credible alternative, an alternative without which your initial challenge would never be taken seriously.

'But why not destroy something and propose nothing?' I ask. 'Why erect something on each and every bare bit of land?'

'Action that is not simply a reaction,' says Chiara. 'As humans, we find such a thing practically impossible to imagine.'

I nod. Chiara and Stephan both gaze fixedly at the dam.

I'm getting rid of this because it is in the way. And anything that replaces it will also be in the way. Or: *There was once an event, and, a long time later, another event, but the two had nothing to do with one another.*

Back at my desk I estimate the amount by which the temperature of the river will drop once the dam is demolished. I settle on an average of one and a half degrees, depending on the season and the expected increase in the temperature of the entire Alpine region in the coming years. Stephan sends me an invite for a symposium in Milan. I write long bits of text in a Word document that I have titled internship.doc. My head is spinning with all the graphs and pie charts. I decide to go out that weekend.

13.

At the holiday park, one of the other Dutch guests comes up to me. She's got her hood up. The drawstrings are pulled so tight that I can only see her nose and mouth. She asks me if I'd like to help organise a bingo night in the activities hall by the park restaurant. In the absence of a bingo mill she's written numbers on the back of Scrabble tiles that she'll put in a big saucepan. Her children will make the bingo cards.

'It looks like it'll be a rainy holiday,' she sighs. 'We'd better take matters into our own hands.'

The weather is no longer really just weather, says British philosopher Timothy Morton. It has become an expression of climate. I thank the woman kindly, but I'm going to be out walking this weekend, despite the rain. I turn and make my way back over the soggy sand path to my little cabin. I notice that the mud is being washed away, exposing the roots of the surrounding trees.

The weather was once an everyday phenomenon, a coincidental circumstance that happily did not tend to present itself as a topic of conversation. Today, it has a more defined character. The weather was once a reason to stay home. Today, it's a reason to take to the streets, to protest.

A WALK

Sometimes it seems as though the compartments on the cable car are hanging motionless but if you look closely it appears they are in fact always moving: a new little car consistently emerges from the mist surrounding the boarding station.

Once in the lift, I can clearly see how the white foam of fast-moving water flows from behind every large rock in the valley. Fortunately, the rain soon dissolves into a fine drizzle, and the drizzle into a low-hanging mist. When I emerge from the mountainside station I am greeted by two marmots who look terrified to see me. They disappear behind a rock.

The route I'm following is marked out by red signs nailed to tree trunks. It is one of the most travelled routes in the area and yet there's no one around just now. After carefully dodging the first two muddy puddles, I decide to give in to the poor condition of the mountain path. If I keep up a decent pace I'll manage twenty-two kilometres before dark, including time for a short break.

After just a few minutes I can hear only the birds in the trees, and now and then some raindrops. The mud splatters reach all the way up to my thighs. 'I don't need anyone here,' I say loudly, speaking into the silence. I mean it: the view and the scent of wet firs are enough. As though to underscore my point, I put my phone on flight mode. By making contact with Robin impossible, the Robin in my head becomes sufficient.

There is an essay by Peter Handke titled 'Essay on the Successful Day', in which he writes that for a day to be considered successful it doesn't have to have been perfect. This is something we often forget. After all, how many times in our lives can we say we've had a perfect day? Once a year, maybe, and mainly in our youth, I would think. And even on these rare occasions I believe that we may have been speaking of successful as opposed to so-called perfect days.

I think about Handke's essay as I pick up a long branch from the ground to use as a walking stick. The essay contains no answers. Has today passed the test? Has it been successful? I don't know. The last day I feel I could call successful with any certainty was the day I was handed my degree certificate. At the same time, that evening I sat in a theatre unable to think about anything other than atomic bombs. It was in fact the first in a series of days in which I felt unsuccessful, and I'm not even sure whether that feeling has come to an end.

For a day to be deemed a success, it shouldn't need to contain anything explicitly pertaining to our ideas of success. Perhaps any day in which nothing noteworthy happens can be called successful. Those days are necessary if we are to string together the events of the days that do stay in our memories. The days when nothing remarkable happens have a function, which is to simply act as a day, and this they fulfil.

Sometimes I think that even a successful day is consumed by other, earlier days, days on which you were with me, for example, and in that case the successful day is reduced to more or less a nothing kind of a day: *Ah not much, just sat around the house, hung up some washing, called the pharmacy* . . . But you were here yesterday, and that's why I deem today a successful day. It might be a successful week, in fact, even if I catch the flu tomorrow or receive yet another tax request from Revenue and Customs.

As I walk past a meadow containing goats, I fantasise that on one of these mountains or in one of these valleys, I own a house. A house to which I can travel each summer to escape the rush of the city. A small house that would feel big, and with a garden that would spill over into the forest.

There would be a family gathering in the house, the gathering of a family that is far bigger than mine. It would be your family, perhaps. Because you're there too, of course, in the house, sitting beside an open fire. And, except for the knowledge that you'll stay there until you drift slowly into sleep, I don't require anything of you. You're already falling, I can see, your head resting heavily on two large cushions.

At night we have sex. The family, which I can now say with certainty is yours, mustn't hear us. This turns us on. After we've had sex, we sleep very deeply, a sleep from which nothing can rouse us. Maybe wild animals have been walking around the house all night – foxes, badgers, deer – but the shadows they cast on the curtains have gone unnoticed.

Is the above scenario a perfect or a successful one? Handke's essay cannot tell me either way.

The days I *am* confident in deeming successful are the days on which I am able to communicate accurately what I am thinking, on which I feel I am able to be myself and have total control over every sound that leaves my throat, every letter I press down on the keyboard. This feeling, the feeling of having a complete mastery over language, might be called inspiration. It is a powerful feeling.

But, as with all things powerful, this feeling has a flipside, something that corrupts it. Having total control over what you say makes you intolerant of your environment (or perhaps your environment intolerant of you), by which I mean that, if every thought you have, every movement you make, every word that leaves your mouth appears to hold infinite meaning, it becomes impossible to attach meaning to the things that others say. As a result, you are left with the feeling that you will forever be alone with the words you write down. A successful day can have the following disastrous conse-quences: in inspiration exists the feeling that the boundaries between yourself and the outside world are dissolving, and their dissolution is one thing, but how are you to re-establish them? Some people become so self-involved, so introverted, that they are left with only colours and shapes before their eyes, no more objects or events. It's crazy that the feeling that you can express absolutely anything (inspiration) can at the same time ensure that you can't say anything at all.

Back home. On closer inspection, the paint is peeling, there is woodworm in the beams. The cushions have fallen from the couch and are now lying on the floor. You and your family left with the northern sun.

Maybe a successful day is for me the kind of day on which I do not have to be fearful (of decay, of coming home to an empty house), or a day on which the possibility of a fear-free existence suddenly presents itself: just the prospect of this makes those days on which I am fearful more bearable. A poem that first managed to put that possibility into words for me is the following, 'For No Clear Reason' by Robert Creeley:

> I dreamt last night
> the fright was over, that
> the dust came, and then water,
> and women and men, together
> again, and all was quiet
> in the dim moon's light.
>
> A paean of such patience –
> laughing, laughing at me,
> and the days extend over
> the earth's great cover,

>   grass, trees, and flower-
>
>   ing season, for no clear reason.

When I recite this in my head, I hear the long-suffering words of a hymn. To be precise, the poem itself is that paean, and it is due to this that I am able to endure today. A day which, however much I have tried simply to take a quiet walk, has already produced necessary struggle. The poem allows me to endure myself.

While songs frequently describe the feeling of a successful day, films and novels seldom do so. That is both strange (I want to read about that feeling) and logical: a successful day does not offer the kind of narrative that films and novels require. But maybe you could make a film about someone who just a few hours before has seen her love and therefore moves effortlessly through the ensuing days, or write a book about someone who after months of grief finally goes back to her nine-to-five job with renewed focus?

. . . was the day on which you got the idea to write an essay about the successful day itself a successful day? Handke asks himself. The response to that question is undoubtedly a yes.

You don't consider the successful day on an off-day, though you might think about the perfect day. Every question you ask yourself begins with *what should happen* and not *what is happening* . . . The difference between the two lies in the fact that a perfect day is something you have to seek out, to make happen, while a successful day is something that finds you. You offer no resistance.

But what if I deem it a successful day because you were there, and you're no good for me? Could you yet become good for me?

14.

On the way to the climate symposium in Milan, while Stephan and Chiara talk about the dam's demolition, I am in the back seat working out, on a scrap of paper, how long I can continue to live on my savings if they aren't topped up. A little over four months, I figure, providing there are no unforeseen expenses. So, around halfway through winter all my money will be gone. I fold up the bit of paper and think of ways to save. Maybe Robin and I could move in together. I could sublet my apartment to earn a little extra money. I'm startled by the thought: why am I not already subletting it?

The symposiums I attended while studying were all heavily subsidised affairs that took place in either old national monuments or brand new university buildings. Compared to these, the building we're now entering is pretty dingy. Most of the walls are covered with posters of unfamiliar Italian pop and rock bands. It's full in the hall: some people are sitting on the floor. Many different languages are being spoken around me. A woman with a pile of papers under her arm appears on stage, and, within a few moments, everyone falls silent.

'The climate crisis,' she begins, 'is caused by the fact that we have, for centuries, practised an anthropocentric science. The human consciousness continually emerges as a kind of sacred entity to which all things and all animals must submit. Western science claims total objectivity but is based on the idea that humankind exists on a plane beyond the objectivity on which its own theories are staked. Even though we have now known for centuries that humankind is not the centre of the universe, we continue to place ourselves in that central position, based solely on the fact that we are both able to think about what is taking place around us and to make known that thinking, the ideas it produces. *Water can't feel its temperature rising, polar bears don't think about their survival, glaciers have no agenda.* These are the words of those who do not care that nature is disappearing. *But we do think about these things, and this gives us priority.* According to some scientists, the result of this kind of thinking is that we have entered a new geological epoch: the Anthropocene. An epoch which follows the Holocene and in which humankind has an essential and lasting influence on the Earth and its climate. In the 4.5 billion years that the Earth has existed, nothing like this has occurred before. The Holocene lasted almost twelve thousand years, the Pleistocene around 2.5 million – how long will the Anthropocene last? Even if humankind were to become extinct tomorrow, the impact we've had on the climate would still outlast us for thousands, maybe even hundreds of thousands of years.'

She pauses and looks around the room. Behind her a screen has descended and is now showing the various layers of the Earth. She continues: 'Even though our consciousness allows us to think in terms of subjects and objects, a system in which objects are usually subordinated to subjects, the degree to which said consciousness can be reduced to chemical processes in the brain is also becoming increasingly clear. In other words: consciousness is itself a matter of tiny objects. It's about time that we understood the consequences of this. We are far less special than we think. Human consciousness is made up of the same elementary particles as the chairs on which you are sitting, as the trees in the rainforest, as the plastics floating in our oceans.'

I am staring at the three circles on the PowerPoint presentation behind her. *Object Oriented Ontology – OOO.* Her speech makes me think of the love I had for objects when I was little. I had always interpreted this love as the expression of a nascent materialism, or in any case a nascent misanthropy. But perhaps it was simply a sincere reverence for the things in my room? I wonder about the extent to which her theory regarding the right to exist is based on the fact that it can be so beautifully summed up via three little zeros.

The second speaker, a friendly-looking middle-aged man, walks onto the stage. He drinks some water from a bottle before placing it on the floor in front of him. 'One of the greatest problems with climate change is that it is so elusive. It is everywhere, it will not be isolated, and so no traditional scientific methods can be applied to it. You cannot place "the climate" under a microscope. Politicians, who have no desire to find solutions to the problem, like to make good use of this. It is of great benefit to them that this phenomenon remains opaque. Complexity makes for intangibility: just look at the governing bodies in which those same politicians have seats, or the complex financial products (such as options and futures contracts) that were recently the root cause of a global economic crisis. As long as a problem is complex or vague, it is difficult to identify the culprits. There is no point in speaking about "the climate", because – well, what exactly are we talking about? In the nineties we at least had the hole in the ozone layer, something that most people could imagine, and which allowed them to care, to worry. The hole is still there, of course, only no one speaks about it any more.

'This problem of opacity is further encouraged by environmental activists. Instead of looking for ways to make global warming visible and tangible, they constantly threaten imminent apocalypse. *What are you waiting for? Act now.* But at the same time: *It's already too late.* These imperatives to immediate action lead to nothing more than fearmongering and gesture politics, to a guilt that paralyses and impedes real action.'

Yes, I think, that's how I feel whenever talk turns to Earth's rising temperature. I feel guilty, don't know where to begin, think about how I should have begun a long time ago, and these feelings paralyse me. I feel like someone who has stopped opening her bills – day after day the climate leaves an unopened letter on my doormat: *You're too late!* is what will be written there if I do open the post. On my dining table, the envelopes stack up. Soon, the dykes will open and claim the contents of my home.

Next to me, Chiara is taking notes. So as not to be left behind I reach in my bag and pull out my own notebook.

'But how then to engage with the problem of global warming?' continues the man, his forehead getting ever sweatier. 'Shouldn't we just come up with a really smart, tech-based solution? Someone like Bill Gates invests millions into artificial climate solutions – research into the possibilities of injecting sulphates in the stratosphere, for example. Wait, let me explain a bit more about that. Whenever an enormous volcano erupts, volcanic ash – sulphates – remain in the stratosphere. This dust blocks the sun's rays and temporarily lowers the Earth's temperature. This phenomenon is known as a "volcanic winter". The last one took place in 1991, following the eruption of Mount Pinatubo in the Philippines. So much micro-dust ended up in the stratosphere that the average global temperature went down by half a degree. And so now the potential to model this effect is being explored. That sounds good, right? But there are many drawbacks. One problem is that it would be impossible to conduct a localised test, and there is no way to assess the results of such a test worldwide without simply trying it out . . . worldwide. And then you're taking quite the risk. It's true that volcanic eruptions block out the sun's rays, but they're also known to have a negative effect on the ozone layer. It was an even bigger eruption about a hundred years earlier – that of the Indonesian Krakatoa in 1883 – that first drew our attention to the greenhouse effect. And even if the artificial volcanic ash did have the desired outcome, you'd have to go on producing it forever. Otherwise the temperature would at once jump back to where it was before – the consequences would be dramatic. Other options currently under research are the introduction of reflective particles into the oceans, which would cause them to reflect more sunlight, and painting the deserts white. I repeat: painting the deserts white.'

An indignant murmur spreads through the hall. I feel my phone vibrate inside my bag and see I've got a message from Robin. *Doing a PhD is truly the most terrible thing a person can put themselves through*, it says. Her supervisor has just rejected the first chapter of her thesis. I text back saying I'll call her as soon as I can. I return my attention to the podium.

'Geoengineering is, in short, not a solution to the problem but just another expression of the human arrogance that underlies it. Instead of hoping for a technological wonder that might in due course rescue us from climate change, we must, first and foremost, stop regarding everything non-human as inferior. You may wish to fight climate change against all costs in the name of saving humankind, but to do so ignores the fact that it is precisely this kind of "humanity-is-everything" thinking that caused it in the first place. In addition, we must acknowledge that, however vague and complex, climate change is itself also an object. An object that is capable of destroying us all.'

15.

'Are you on your phone again, Ida?' Chiara asks me on the way back. Stephan has stayed behind in Milan. I'm hungry and want to suggest we stop at a roadside restaurant, but then I remember Chiara's strict veganism.

'I'm trying to stay in contact with my friends in the Netherlands,' I respond. My friends in the Netherlands have almost all set their emails to out-of-office autoreply because they're soaking up the sun on some Asian beach or on a road trip in Eastern Europe. Carl has posted two photos of the house in the Ardennes where he and his friends are holidaying. In one of the photos is a wine cellar, in the other an enormous four-poster bed. A few posts further back, my mother is asking her friends – who, like her, are ageing hippies

– which are the most beautiful spots in Ibiza. At the top of my screen, a message arrives from Robin. She's managed to find someone else to cheer her up, thanks very much.

'Less than a month to go now,' says Chiara, 'and we'll have made great progress towards restoring the natural order of things.'

16.

In books and films love is often portrayed as immense, compelling, infinite. Suddenly, a woman enters the room (often, she is wearing a dress; often, the dress is red). She whips her hair round a few times, orders a drink at the bar, lights a Gauloise, and within two weeks she and the protagonist (who, in the books, is often never quite handsome enough to be with the woman in question, but who in the films must always be) have given up their old lives in order to be together. Forever. Then, a war breaks out. The couple find themselves on a sinking cruise ship. Or else a colony of murderous aliens lands on Earth, putting the couple's love to the test. The love transpires to be strong enough, even when one of the two meets a sticky end.

The reality is different. The reality comprises a whole load of misinterpreted text messages. The reality is that there are very few people who truly suit a red dress, and that it's a pretty big deal to ask someone to give up their entire life or to change for someone you've known for just a few months, though we may well expect that of one another (mine and Robin's first dates took place in the cinema, and yes, those films have a lot to answer for). The reality is that you probably wouldn't run all the way back down to the lower deck to save me, you're not crazy, you're already in the lifeboat, and I'm not about to take on those aliens who've just dragged you into their spaceship. Instead, I go into hiding.

An idea: a film in which an argument of epic proportions takes place, in which one member of the couple slams their way out of the scene, or else bursts into laughter. Or, and I'm just riffing here, a scene in which someone gets angry simply because their blood sugar is low, in which nothing else is really the matter.

ON THE REVOLUTIONS OF THE HEAVENLY SPHERES

In one of Leopardi's essays, the one about Copernicus, the first hour of the day (let's say, around eight in the morning) enters into discussion with the sun. The sun, a great, grumbling ball of light, has on that day decided that he no longer has any desire to move around the Earth. For the characters in this essay, the Earth is of course at the centre of everything: century after century the sun has orbited around us. But he's had enough. He's on strike.

Sun: *I'm sick of always going around in circles just to shed light on a few tiny creatures living on a handful of mud. Tonight I have decided that I will no longer be doing my rounds. If the humans want to see light, they should make a fire, or come up with something else.*

The first hour of the day, the moment at which dawn breaks, is distraught. If the sun no longer wishes to come up, he himself is in danger: without the sun, no sunrise, and without the sunrise, no first hour of the day. In the end, the sun commands the last hour of the day to descend to Earth and to convince some scientist to do something to make it so that the Earth moves around the sun. If the sun will no longer move, then the Earth must be called to action, otherwise one half of the Earth will from now on live in infinite darkness, the other half in infinite daylight. It's a fine solution for the sun, who stands to benefit greatly from it.

The scientist to whom the last hour of the day subsequently pays a visit is Nicolaus Copernicus, who has already noticed that the sun has not risen on time. He is worried, and he travels to the sun in search of clarification. He explains that he fears the people of Earth will have no desire to give up their position at the centre. He doubts, too, whether he can play a significant role. Maybe if he was Hercules or Roland, instead of a weedy Catholic priest . . .

Sun: *What does that have to do with anything? Were we not told that an ancient mathematician* once said that, were he able to move beyond the world, he could shift heaven and*

---

* Leopardi is alluding here to Archimedes, who claimed that, if he had an enormously long crowbar and a fixed point outside the Earth, he could pop the Earth out of orbit in no time. Today, an outsider perspective is known as an Archimedean perspective, a perspective from which you can consider everything in its totality, which is to say that distance establishes independence, a divine perspective, from which you can make universal statements about the world. But to make such universal statements, without being part of the universe itself, is relatively difficult.

Earth? If you're anywhere near as clever as that old man, you should be able to mobilise your planet.

Copernicus can jump high and low, present any argument that occurs to him – the sun knows how to refute them all. His last argument is that he fears he will be ostracised. As a priest he knows too well the consequences of challenging a biblical worldview. But the sun stands firm and makes a prediction. Namely, that Copernicus will not find himself in trouble, and that he will write a book on the subject dedicated to the Pope. With that, this section comes to an end, and the reader knows: from now on, the Earth will move around the sun.

Dedicating his book *On the Revolutions of the Heavenly Spheres* to the Pope in the hope of reducing his chances of excommunication – that is precisely what Copernicus in fact did. What he did not know, of course, was that the reason he would not be ostracised was because he would die just days following the book's publication. He would indeed never have to pay for his thoughts – Galileo Galilei would do that for him about a hundred years later.

In Leopardi's essay the sun finds a very practical solution to the Earth's geocentrism, ensuring that the Earth be forced to give up her central role, and that's that. In reality it would take much longer for Copernicus's discovery to be accepted. Only in 1835 would the Catholic Church remove his work from the list of forbidden books.

But the end of *geo*centrism would not signal the end of *ego*centrism. Even when humankind had, on the whole, come to understand itself as no longer occupying the centre of the universe, most individuals would still see themselves as the centres of their universes. Everyone is forever doomed to egocentrism, because everyone is, simply put, the centre of their own world. It is impossible to look at the world through another's eyes, however empathetic you might be.

You can imagine why the discovery that the Earth was not the centre of the universe led to panic: humankind went from main character to sidekick in a split second. In addition to which, a whole load of new questions were raised: where does the universe end? Is there another centre somewhere? Does God exist? The universe offered no answers.

The eternal silence of these infinite spaces terrifies me, wrote Blaise Pascal of the situation in his *Pensées*, or, *Thoughts*. It is a sentence that haunts my brain on an almost daily basis.

This is because I understand it so well, I suspect, even though it was written almost four centuries ago. Sometimes just walking down a quiet street is enough to terrify me. How must Pascal have felt standing before a newly discovered, infinitely vast and silent universe?*

Once Copernicus had proven that mankind was not the centre of the universe and thus, in all likelihood, not the apple of God's eye, something had to be devised in order to quell the anxiety this had provoked; to ensure, at the very least, mankind's exceptional role on the Earth. *We might not be the most important creatures in the universe, but we are the most unique!* On the basis of the nature of their scientific findings (*Who else could do this!*), humans were able to take courage.

Thus the focus on the human consciousness grew: by blowing the question of the highest good out of the water

---

* The idea of an infinite and immense silence fascinated Leopardi, too. Only, for him, this silence was not due to the existence of an infinite universe in which no one was supplying answers, but due to the possibility of the absence of everything – including the universe. Further, Leopardi was not frightened by this silence, but rather saw it as an ideal. Because he believed everything was evil (*That is to say, everything that is, is evil . . . The only good is nonbeing*), infinite silence was for him the highest thing attainable. Ideally, silence was for him not the absence of sound but the lack of anything that could create noise.

with the question of what distinguishes people from animals and objects, humankind could once again congratulate itself on its uniqueness. The success of Descartes, who demonstrated the existence of the individual consciousness and its centrality to the acquisition of knowledge, strikes me as no coincidence. According to Descartes, animals were nothing more than machines. Animals, he said, have no soul and no feelings – they're sort of like vending machines. Later philosophers would attribute consciousness to animals, but not self-*awareness*: the consciousness of being in possession of consciousness.

Descartes' *Cogito, ergo sum* (I think, therefore I am) itself constituted a prelude to the distinction between subject and object that would from then on form the basis of the whole of Western science and philosophy. The only thing that I know exists for certain is that within me that thinks, according to Descartes. This thinking element he dubbed the spirit, and it existed, according to Descartes, completely separately from the body. The spirit was disembodied and the domain of consciousness; the body, on the other hand, was material, and it belonged with the objects. It was the spirit that made us human and allowed us to register and consider that which occurred in the world of objects.

This Cartesian dichotomy between subject and object had far-reaching effects: seeing to it, for example, that people no longer viewed themselves as a component of nature. Nature was the domain of objects. And it was up to humankind, cultural beings in possession of minds as well as bodies, to come to understand and to control nature.

But what does it mean to know reality, precisely as it is? What is it that allows us to know a tree as a tree? The tree itself, purely through its existence, you might think. But you could also say that the tree is only a tree because humankind defines it as such, and in that case it's us who make a tree a tree. The tree appears to us a certain way, and we in turn recognise in it the qualities that enable us to call what we see 'tree'.

It was Immanuel Kant who in his *Critique of Pure Reason* first wrote something like the above. Until then, mankind had tried in vain to locate essence within objects, while the objects themselves revealed nothing. *We must turn this around and assume that meaning exists inside people's heads!* Kant concluded. Consciousness is what gives meaning to objects; even if objects themselves provide our senses with information, it's the human consciousness that affords meaning to the world around us by processing that information via concepts of space, time and causality. Objects only give us the material that sets consciousness to work, organising and comprehending. Nowadays, this is a common line of thinking, but in Kant's time it was radical: until then, consciousness was seen more as a kind of basket in which to arrange the properties of objects. Kant himself dubbed this shift in thought his Copernican revolution.

But in contrast with Copernicus, Kant ensured that humankind would see itself as even more important than before. In saying that nature only possessed meaning in its relation to people, he would enable people to see nature as inferior. The result is the continuing belief that objects are ours for the taking: a bit of land, the rainforests, the oil underground . . . They only mean something because they mean something to us, and so we're entitled to do what we want with them.

It follows that for those philosophers who adhere to an object-oriented mode of thinking, human arrogance enabled and encouraged by Kant's Copernican revolution is one of the primary causes of pollution and the climate crisis now facing us. This arrogance was further strengthened by the success of the natural sciences: suddenly, everything seemed as though it could be manipulated (we even managed to split the atom, the ultimate act of manipulation and human dominance). That our first response to the climate crisis has been to research the possibility of a clever, technology-based solution is a clear indication that this arrogance is not in decline.

To tackle such arrogance we need to abolish the distinction between culture and nature, writes the French philosopher Quentin Meillassoux. The world this would establish is what he calls 'the Great Outdoors', a world in which human consciousness no longer plays a role, or, at least, not a key role. In the Great Outdoors, people and nature are of equal worth. On the one hand, this would mean accepting that objects do not require humans in order to create meaningful relationships (think, for example, of a tree that is struck by lightning, or a tsunami that sinks an island); on the other, that human consciousness can also be reduced to a number of objects (neurones, atoms, quarks). In the Great Outdoors, everything, even the things created by humans, as well as humans themselves, has meaning in and of itself – not because of humans' assigning of meaning through language and/or science. This would lead to a world without hierarchies. This equalising of humans and nature could lead, among other things, to objects – those that are currently perceived as such – being afforded rights. This is something that has already been attempted – with the rain-forests in South America, for example; or in New Zealand, where there is a river that has been given rights. Who knows, perhaps one day animals and plants will be attributed what we currently call 'human rights'.

If we are to imagine a world in which people are no more important than anything else, it might help to picture what would happen to the Earth if humankind were to disappear. This is what Weisman does in *The World Without Us*. In a world without people, anything can happen. Similarly, Meillassoux imagines an Earth that *precedes* the existence of humans: what was the reality of a time before humans? And what can we learn from it?

It is pretty difficult to see the world around us as a place on which we do not have to impose meaning. To admit that objects lead their own lives, that they engage in meaningful relationships with others and among themselves, is to admit that there is a world on which we, as humans, bear no influence, and so have no control. For a being that has considered itself to be superior to everything for centuries now, this is an uncomfortable realisation.

The Earth wouldn't care if it all went to shit, say climate sceptics, *so why not just continue as we are?* It's true, of course: just like the sun in that essay by Leopardi, the Earth regards us with total indifference. Humankind cannot survive without the Earth, but the Earth itself has absolutely no need of us.

This thought is fear-inducing. Just as fear-inducing as the knowledge that the Earth, our planet, is not the centre of the universe and never was. And in that fear we can perhaps identify the reason that many people do not take the climate crisis seriously. Of course, you could take the fact that humans have succeeded in pushing their own habitat to the brink of total destruction as evidence of how powerful we are (*We can even influence the climate!*), but you must then at the same time admit that we have created a problem for which we are most likely unable to locate a solution.

And thus: fear. Nobody wants to be powerless. When someone is powerless, they are unimportant. Imagine that you were the only person left on the Earth, the last sorry little Cartesian huddling around a fire: whatever thought you might have, it wouldn't matter to anyone. That would make you feel incredibly lonely, because what is loneliness if not the deeply upsetting realisation that you don't mean anything to anyone? Nothing terrifies us quite as much as the possibility of our own insignificance.*

What it comes down to is that humankind, as a whole, is lonely. We cannot stand that no one says anything back, that those damn objects do not respond to the meaning with which we imbue them, that we have never heard animals speak – well, perhaps every now and then in the form of those shrill screams that fill our slaughterhouses, but never with words, never with solutions for the things that have preoccupied us for so long. Even heaven is empty. And so we put ourselves out by annihilating all of that wordless nature around us, like a desperate lover who receives no message back and so drinks themselves silly in the local bar.

The eternal silence of these infinite spaces terrifies me.

Get a dog, you might say to Pascal. Go for a walk. But Pascal gets a new car, a super slim, lightweight phone and some shares in artificial volcanic ash.

---

* Kierkegaard noted that we are so frightened of loneliness we can only conceive of it in terms of punishment for criminals.

I enjoy thinking about all these philosophers, people like Leopardi and Kant and Copernicus who existed and who became angry or frightened or amused. But recently, I am more and more convinced that history is as much a history of objects as of people. Apples that fell from trees and either rotted or were eaten, mountains that in the winter were coated in a thick layer of snow, swords that killed kings, atom bombs that exploded, enormous ships that did and did not reach faraway continents, fluttering flags, great floods, grains of wheat, tombstones.

17.

Before I go to the airport to pick up Robin, I drive to the nearest town to buy a couple of bottles of good wine. What makes a good wine I do not know, and so I buy the most expensive bottles I can afford. Because the rain is torrential, I duck into a church on my way back from the shop to my parking spot. I trip over the church's threshold on the way in but manage to keep myself upright.

I look around me, at the wooden benches and at the dark stained-glass windows. It smells like wet stone and mildew. Just as when I watch old black-and-white films and find it difficult to imagine the world of the early 1900s as containing colour, I find it difficult to think that those who were alive in the Renaissance weren't exposed to the stench of centuries-old churches on every street corner, churches that in fact must have then smelled of brand new plasterwork. My mobile informs me that Robin's flight has a one-hour delay.

Tables with candles on them have been set up at various points throughout the church. Only one of the candles is lit. The sole sound I can hear is the dim patter of raindrops on the large windows, the only person the cleaner who is mopping the stone floor along the church's nave. The marble tiles shine in the spots he's just wiped. I sit down on one of the pews and look up. The saints on the frescos form a procession of encircled heads.

Behind the altar, set about three metres or so above the ground, is an organ. The instrument appears wholly neglected. If someone were to push down on one of its keys, it looks as though it would only creak and groan. Organ music sounds most beautiful in a church: the reverberations enabled by the high ceilings give it an extra dimension. The higher notes form the melody that reaches your ears from all corners of the church, while it seems as though the lower tones, the tones that the organist also plays with their feet, are palpable to those who cannot strictly hear – which is to say, everyone buried beneath the church floor. If you consider the corpses surrounding you the moment the organ opens up its registers, the music is afforded a new charge. In comparison with the footwork, the high, hand-played notes sound naïve; in comparison with the dead, the living come across as tenuous, hysterical.

The most beautiful organ music was written by Bach and Handel, who were born a month apart, both in Germany: Handel in Halle and Bach in Eisenach (the reverse would not have sounded quite as nice). Just two hours apart by car, if there had been cars then.

18.

As I drive into the parking area, I see Robin in the distance, already standing in front of arrivals. She's smoking and wearing a long dress under her dark blue raincoat. It's good to see her in the flesh again. We hold each other for a while, and then I throw her bags into the boot. It takes a minute before I can get the car started. I'm blushing.

That evening I get us pizza from the restaurant at the resort. Robin tells me that she's been invited to speak at a conference. She wants to accept the invite, but she can only do so if her supervisor approves her most recent chapter redrafts. I take a bite of my quattro stagioni. A piece of artichoke drops onto my trousers. The two bottles of wine I bought are finished in under one and a half hours.

Robin gestures to the bundle of papers lying on the floor next to the bed.

'What's that?'

'I've written a few things down these past weeks,' I reply, and push the papers under the bed with my foot. Robin takes off her dress and lets it fall on the mattress. 'Let's do something fun tomorrow,' I say, pushing myself against her naked body. 'What do you feel like? We could go canoeing?'

In the middle of the night I awake from a dream in which thousands, maybe tens of thousands of salmon have stormed and occupied the research centre because they no longer want to do what it is salmon must do after the dam is brought down: i.e., swim for days against the current of the river in order to procreate somewhere high up in the mountains. The regional government originally suggested digging up the dam slowly, carefully, instead of demolishing it. Explosives are a great deal cheaper, according to Stephan, but he fears that the animals in the surrounding environment will be affected by the blast for weeks. I ask myself whether the animals will appreciate it if we remove the dam. What if they're all happy with having their comings and goings limited? If animals possess consciousness, they can surely also be susceptible to Stockholm syndrome?

19.

The canoe hire is on a wide bank on the side of a river, which, in warmer summers, is likely a hotspot for holidaymakers. Here and there are crushed, empty cans and litre boxes of wine. The canoe guy is in his thirties, short and muscular. He explains to us in broken English that he's happy to see us, that he's not done good business this year. Robin responds in Italian, and I cannot follow the conversation that unfolds after this. The man walks us over to a shed filled with canoes (as well as motorbikes, fishing equipment, life jackets) and gestures towards a yellow two-person boat. In one way or another, I have the idea that yellow is the colour all canoes should be, even though I cannot recall having ever sat in a yellow canoe, and so I am satisfied.

As well as being deeper, the river is wider and rougher than usual. In the canoe, we swing side to side, moving tensely downstream for a hundred metres or so, until the shed is no longer in view and we give in to the current. The sun has broken through, and I'm enjoying the sound of rushing water, the sight of the mountains that tower over us left and right, the slopes filled with birds and flowers. The two moles on Robin's neck are looking at me. Above them are the downy hairs that lead up to the birthmark at the base of her skull. The paddling makes us hot, and we take off our jackets. Through the course of the morning, the number of walkers following our route increases rapidly, and we sail past river-banks full of people. Where have they all appeared from so suddenly? Where have they all been these last few weeks?

It's a challenging trip; we have to get used to this new way of moving. Every now and then one of us pushes a paddle against an exposed rock to keep the canoe from tipping over. We pass under an overhanging tree and get caught in its long vines. I carefully untangle them from Robin's hair with one arm while protecting my face from the leafy tentacles with the other.

'Why did we take a two-person canoe again? Two one-person canoes would have been much easier, you're always going at a different rhythm to me.'

'You were there too,' I reply. I move my upper body to the right to keep my balance, which nearly pushes Robin overboard.

'If we'd had two separate canoes, we'd at least be able to save one another.'

A little further on the river becomes calmer. We don't have to do much more than keep still and wait for the water to carry us along. We are silent. Out of a growing boredom, I start to pluck leaves from the low-hanging branches. We moor up around midday. I take a paper bag containing sandwiches out of my bag as I set a foot back on land.

'I think we should break up.' Robin whispers it, but I hear her clearly.

'What?' I lose my balance, prop myself up with the paddle I'm still holding.

'I've fallen in love with someone else,' she says, louder now. To avoid looking at me, she fixes on the canoe, which we're now trying to pull up onto land together.

I start crying.

'And you want to keep seeing her?' I ask, just to be sure.

20.

A noise like static starts up, as though someone's put on a playlist of sounds of the sea. Robin takes a sip from a carton of apple juice and looks at the ground. A lock of her hair falls over her eyes, and with her free hand she moves it away. It's difficult to tell whether or not she is crying.

'I'm sorry,' she says.

I stare at my sandwich. The mozzarella has partially melted and is seeping out at the sides. The sandwich looks sick.

'No,' I say, faltering, 'it's me – I'm sorry.' I take a deep breath. 'Can we fix this?'

Robin shakes her head.

'I'll never be so selfish. Ever again.'

She's been looking down the entire time. Behind her appears another canoe, young parents with two small children between their legs. One of the kids looks as though they're trying to yell something, but no sound comes out.

'What's her name?' I ask. My voice is lost in the noise that is only getting louder, as though someone somewhere is turning up the volume. Maybe the noise is just in my head. Maybe I've finally gone mad.

Robin looks up. She points, stunned, to something going on behind me. I turn around. My mouth drops open and the sandwich falls out of my hand, the mozzarella merging willingly with the sand by our feet. It takes a minute before I am able to grasp what it is I am seeing.

21.

An enormous tidal wave has appeared on the horizon.

The dam at the reservoir has given way, releasing a wall of water.

22.

Above us, birds fly away from the treetops. Rabbits and deer shoot along the hills. I begin to run upwards, my feet moving over the stones as though they're hot coals. After just a few steps I lose my aqua socks. The sand I'm kicking away with the soles of my feet is flying around Robin's ears. 'Come on,' I shout. Perhaps she can't hear me; the noise has become unbearably loud.

23.

About five metres or so below Ida, the water catches up with Robin, and she falls. Behind her: trees, shrubs, canoes. A little further away, about ten metres: the young family, trying to get ashore. Ida looks back at them, and then at Robin.

IDA: Four hundred million years ago an animal first crawled onto land, and here you all are, crawling onto land. Come here, come here next to me and stay.

(She has never said this to anyone before.) Bits of earth crumble away, expose roots.

IDA: Four hundred thousand years ago humankind first decided to cook their food, which meant that their bowels required less energy, which meant that their brains could grow.

Robin's big, lovely head is getting smaller by the millisecond. The foam slurps it up, sucks her away.

IDA: Our brains grew bigger and bigger. Fourteen thousand years ago a person first took in a dog as a house pet. Five thousand years later, a cat.

Every living thing is swallowed by the shockwaves. Ida looks around.

IDA: Above me, the bats and owls are fleeing; beneath me, the salamanders and water rats. For me, there's nowhere to go.

In the end even light disappears in less than an instant (like two people who leave each other one morning because of what it means to be two people).

IDA: The Earth had to exist for 4.5 billion years before someone finally observed that it was not at the centre of the universe. What's more, that person was ridiculed.

Two tectonic plates move away from each other at lightning speed, forming two worlds.

IDA: And in one, people move around, impoverished, and in the other, they profit from weapons.

shouting: And some of us will be found naked
moaning: And some of us will probably never be found

But everything about me will be new, I think
I will slip right into time, as though it were a second skin
And right into death, too, as though it were a second home

Then an airborne branch strikes Ida's head and at last she loses, you could say, her consciousness.

I HATE THE WATER, I LOVE THE WATER

the idea that tomorrow may never come, not because everything is going to end, but because this moment you're in
right now will go on forever

the fear that you may suddenly realise you're keeping a
massive secret, only you didn't know about it until just now

consenting to trust out of laziness: after all, to distrust means
to take action

the feeling that with each minute you don't speak you're
losing your language: first goes the grammar, then the
adverbs and the adjectives, until, eventually, the consonants
come away like loose teeth. at last, your own name is gone

the illusion of free will: you may choose to live, but this
doesn't mean that you can

how language works: someone who has never been stabbed
understands what a stabbing pain is

wanting language to click and clack, a glockenspiel

to be made of stone – not a stone that feels nothing, but one
which warms in the sun

if this isn't reality, then why do you let the things beyond it
affect you so much?

a mathematician in a world without numbers

time heals; time alienates

the silence of dusk

the pure noise of us

TWO GAPS

you take to the sea to smack down the waves
you're looking for somewhere safe to hole up but you
mine the zone with dynamite

you skip as a mode of escape
you dive into the deep, which appears
shallow, crashing against the bottom

you hide behind visibility
you wish every word were onomatopoeic
you rattle whenever you stumble

Every now and then I find it kind of sad for my double bed
that, in the past ten years, I've shared it with someone else
a maximum of one hundred times; I have slept on it alone
over three thousand times. Why did I even buy a two-person
bed? Was it a promise to myself that in the near future
I'd be waking up each morning next to another person?
Whatever the case, I had the feeling, while dragging the
heavy double mattress into my twelve-square-metre room in
student accommodation, that something fundamental had
changed. But I might as well have bought an air mattress:

it wasn't until two moves later that the double bed finally came in handy.

Recently, while getting dressed, whenever I grab one of the many creased items from the chair on which I toss my clothes in the evening and look over at my empty, unmade bed, I think of my first days on the double mattress. I had big expectations – but of what, exactly? I had ambitions in the realm of love, despite knowing nothing about relationships, let alone long-term relationships, or being aware of the fact that even a mutual infatuation will subside, given time.

My diary from that period:

> I love possibility, which is a thought that I can justify by saying that I believe it is a brave thing: to love that which is uncertain, to leave your options open. I like the not-knowing, the grey areas. But above all I like the mountains and the mountains are white. What now? Meanwhile, I'm trying to impress 6 billion people at once.

Today, as I am working out whether my big expectations were met, a sentence from Patricia de Martelaere's essay 'On Saying Nothing; or, The Emperor's New Clothes' comes to mind: *Under every lover lies the empty bed*. This is both a beautiful and a wretched sentence. It indicates that the bed on which you have been lying all night with your beloved will, once they go back home, or perhaps simply to the toilet, become, once again, your own empty one. Not even the love of your life can alter this fact. And even if it's your shared bed, in your shared bedroom, in the apartment whose rent the two of you split equally, it remains thus: we see the bed as the place where our ideal, symbiotic love becomes reality, but when day breaks, everyone goes their own way. This doesn't mean that every love affair is doomed to fail, but it does make clear the unbridgeable gap between you and your beloved, who sometimes leaves a patch of drool on your pillowcase in the mornings. We hope that love will meld us together but quickly realise this is unattainable, that we are wretched. It does, however, indicate that something unattainable is also reassuring. It makes the *absence* of the beloved a little less unbearable, because it places the cause of any failure outside of your self. *Ach*, I say, *under every lover the empty bed*, and pull my duvet firmly towards me, over the untouched half of the mattress.

Pessoa noted:

> I suppose no one truly admits the existence of another person. One might concede that the other person is alive and feels and thinks like oneself, but there will always be

an element of difference, a perceptible discrepancy, that one cannot quite put one's finger on.

But of course, we can never stop ourselves from *trying* to put our finger on it, to make the discrepancy negotiable, articulable. Most of the literature on love is about the way our loves continue to slip through our fingers. (Anne Carson: *Who is the real subject of most love poems? Not the beloved. It is that hole.*) But the language with which you address your lover in order to bridge the gap between you is as arbitrary as the lover herself. Not for nothing is the Patricia de Martelaere phrase *Under every lover the empty bed* in the middle of a treatment on language. De Martelaere compares lovers to writers, because just as the despairing writer tries to find the right words for things that are all but impossible to express for the simple reason that words are words and things are things, the despairing lover will utter, *They could have been anyone.* Whoever considers the distance between themselves and their lover relinquishes that sense of necessity, of urgency, that accompanies the act of loving deeply.

Both language and love are thus concerned with a discrepancy: language must contend with the unbridgeable gap between itself and reality, and love with the unbridgeable gap between lover and beloved. But the two have more similarities: both not only have a hole at the heart of their existence; both exist *by virtue of* that hole. Because, in love, there would be no longing were it not for that hole, and longing is a condition of love's existence, the form in which love most often presents itself, whether it's located in the acute physical desire you experience on first meeting someone, or in the fact that after thirty-five years of marriage you still long for the moment when your wife will get home from work. Were we actually to meld with our beloved, become one, a relationship with them would be impossible. The battle, the distance between lovers, has an obvious function: it makes sure that love does not expire, because it is constantly deferred.

If language would, for her part, become one with the physical realm, rather than standing in for it, she would also become an impossibility, because language, too, exists only in relation to. Language is always about something, and whoever wishes to speak about something must have an outsider's perspective. And then it remains: the words that we choose for the world around us are not necessarily bound to those things that they are meant to describe. Which is why the driving force behind both love and language is the gap.

What's more, the gap of love is enlarged by the gap of language, i.e., when the people you love make use of the fact that there is always a difference between language and reality, a difference that allows them to bend and appropriate your words. Anyone who's ever been in love is aware that the potential for miscommunication in the love dynamic is much greater than in any other kind of human relation. Because so much is at stake, we are disposed to read far too much into someone's words, to locate in those words a new reality, and in this way someone's words can take on their own life. With the baker or the butcher you can be sure that what you say will be taken at its word (four ounces of mince is four ounces of mince), but lovers have the tendency to explain everything to their advantage (or indeed to their disadvantage, which, in a roundabout way, turns it back to their advantage, as is so often the case in disagreements between lovers). Why? Because this is the only way to make bearable the risk of self-sacrifice that accompanies love. And we end up twisting our own words, too, by frequently qualifying the statement we used to wound the other in such a way as to get ourselves off the hook. Conclusion: as soon as we speak, what we say is earmarked for interpretation. The words have already been released and must only be picked up.

In any case, love and language are happy to be paired with one another. Language often adopts love as its subject, and the despairing lover often turns to language as a last resort. In the poem 'Non chiederci la parola' ('Don't ask us the word') by Eugenio Montale, translated by Joseph Cary, this relation is beautifully expressed:

> Don't ask of us the word that squares on every side
> our formless spirit, and in fiery letters
> proclaims it …

Feelings are formless, so you can't expect to be able to trace their edges with words. Whoever attempts this will be swallowed up by cliché, by any number of one-size-fits-all expressions that in reality describe no one and nothing. At best you might be able to drape an old blanket over it, to weave a thin web of language in the hope that someday, some element of your feelings will find itself held there.

Longing is something that we associate with absence, with emptiness. I long for someone because I do not have access to them. To have access to them would fill the empty space – the gap – in me. But is longing necessarily the result of an internal emptiness? The American writer and filmmaker Chris Kraus writes that lack is not the basis of longing – rather, it is founded on a surplus, on an excess of energy.

Kraus regards desire as a kind of claustrophobia within one's own body. When I first read this, I had to think of my four-teen-year-old self, she who brought book after book into her teenage bedroom, desperately searching for something that would divert her attention, for an antidote for loneli-ness. And I think of the self who would, just a few years later, expectantly and with a hunger for life, assemble the double bed she'd just bought. In both instances, it felt as though I contained too much, not too little.

This last corresponds with the experience of longing for something: we will often say that we are about to burst with longing; if longing were to come forth from some gap, some lack inside us, surely the feeling would be more like an implosion? In the case of longing that is generated by a perceived lack, your body is an empty shell, something that will be filled up by that which it covets. But in the case of longing that is caused by excess, you will experience that bursting feeling. The lack that we associate with longing must therefore exist beyond ourselves (in the form of the gap at the heart of love, which is reinforced by the gap at the heart of language); there is nothing missing within.

But is it in fact a lack? Who was it who decided that the space that exists between you and the beloved is an object that stands in the way? Or that that space is necessarily an empty one? If the gap were a vacuum, there would be nothing, practically speaking, standing in the way of your melding together. But then what does this gap, this hole, look like? Is it more like a crater? And if it does contain something, what is it?

I believe that the hole at the heart of love is not in fact empty and its influence is increased by the hole at the heart of language, because *the hole of love exists within the hole of language*. If the two holes were to constitute the two circles in a Venn diagram, the contents of the hole of love would be contained within the much larger, all-encompassing hole of language. The distance between two lovers exists in the fact of their feelings for one another, their *true feelings*, which they can never adequately express. The distance between you and your beloved is made clearest by the way in which they interpret what you have said, but above all in everything you *wish* you'd said, or think you *should* have said, or would like to *have* said – all those unspoken words that influence how you behave towards your lover but of which the lover will remain forever unaware, and that would have surely fallen short of what it was you wanted to communicate anyway. On the one hand, lovers might benefit from a language that would leave less room for open interpretation (if only every word could be onomatopoeic!); on the other, such a language would make the longing of lovers impossible. Above all, such a language is unimaginable.

Yet it is precisely at the moment when we feel the most connected to our lover that we do not require words. When you're having sex, for example, or have just had sex and are now lying entangled on the double bed, and the gap at the heart of love and of language is, for just a moment, at its smallest. At such moments, you do not need language. A successful love is a silent love. But before long you must speak once again to your beloved, must allow the gap to expand, because without it there is no longing, etc. The gaps derive from inadequacy, but it is precisely this inadequacy that makes sure we can love someone for more than an hour. And it's in this way that the gap of love closes, so that it can continually recreate itself, can continue to exist.

Language and love might just as easily be figured in terms of a number of other completely different metaphors. A mountain, a book, a game. Still, I like to think of the two gaps as I undress at night, as I place my clothes one by one back on the chair of discarded garments and nestle all alone into my two-person bed, concluding, satisfied: this gap is safe for now. There is nothing lacking within me.

EVERYWHERE YOU GO YOU FEEL STRONGER

You dream about nuclear explosions. Now and then
you explode with longing. Someone says:
struggle. You hear: loss. Is it possible

you could crawl into the boxing ring and come out
the winner? Neck broken, they raise
your tiny shaking hand into the air. You never
worked this hard to build sandcastles
against the line of the incoming tide before.

Someone says: we're setting sail.
You hear: drowning. Cast buoys of language
instead of raising the boom, *save our souls*
with nautical metaphor.

And every day you are inside every day, wandering
around with a bucket, water sloshing
to the rhythm of your raging heart. The rhythm

of the water running over the edge
of a glass, a crib, seeping now
under a door and into the next room

where you are also sitting. In a chair that falls over
every time you stand up. What does it matter.
Reading a book, with great satisfaction, you can

ignore those who have seen land. No,
not any more. Someone says: quiet, land.
And you who would like to see it this once,

finally ready, helping the passengers
onto the jetty, taking a bag, having long
forgotten that you were once one of them.

You can divide up the rooms today.
Call us into the sun after breakfast.
Come up with something for us to do later.

Maybe we could go sit in the canoe
and wait for the river to take everything away.

Acknowledgements

In the writing of this book, I've made use of the following books/sources:

Carson, Anne, *Eros the Bittersweet*, Princeton University Press, 1986

Creeley, Robert, 'For No Clear Reason', *Selected Poems of Robert Creeley*, University of California Press, 1991

De Martelaere, Patricia, 'Om niets te zeggen, of De nieuwe kleren van de keizer', *Een verlangen naar ontroostbaarheid*, Meulenhoff, 1993

Descartes, René, *Meditations on First Philosophy*, Cambridge University Press, 1996

Duras, Marguerite, *The Malady of Death*, Grove Atlantic, 1986, trans. Barbara Bray

Handke, Peter, 'The Successful Day', *The Jukebox & Other Essays on Storytelling*, Farrar, Straus & Giroux, 1994, trans. Ralph Manheim and Krishna Winston

Harari, Yuval, *Sapiens*, Penguin Books UK, 2015

Kant, Immanuel, *Kant: Critique of Pure Reason*, Cambridge University Press, 1999, trans. Paul Guyer and Allen Wood

Kierkegaard, Søren, *Over de vertwijfeling (De ziekte tot de dood)*, Prisma, 1963, trans. H. A. van Munster and A. P. Klaver

Klein, Naomi, *This Changes Everything*, Penguin Books, 2015

Leopardi, Giacomo, *Operette Morali: Essays and Dialogues*, University of California Press,1982, trans. Giovanni Cecchetti

Leopardi, Giacomo, *Zibaldone*, Farrar, Straus and Giroux, 2017, ed. Michael Caesar, trans. Kathleen Baldwin et al.

McGlynn, Karyna, 'Erin with the Feathered Hair', *I have To Go Back to 1994 and Kill a Girl*, Sarabande Books, 2009

Meillassoux, Quentin, *After Finitude*, Bloomsbury Academic, 2010, trans. Ray Brassier

Mitchell, Joni, cbc-interview met Jian Ghomeshi, 2013, https://www.youtube.com/watch?v=pEJuiZN3jI8

Montale, Eugenio, 'Non chiederci', trans. K. van Eerd

Morton, Timothy, *Hyperobjects: Philosophy and Ecology after the End of the World*, University of Minnesota Press, 2013

Pascal, Blaise, *Pensées and Other Writings*, Oxford University Press, 2008, ed. Anthony Levi, trans. Honor Levi

Pessoa, Fernando, *The Book of Disquiet*, Serpent's Tail, 1991, 2010, ed. Maria José de Lancastre, trans. Margaret Jull Costa

Pirandello, Luigi, *One, None and a Hundred-Thousand*, E. P. Dutton, 2017, trans. Samuel Putnam

Rhys, Jean, *Voyage in the Dark*, Penguin, 2000

Rich, Adrienne, 'Women: Sex and Sexuality', in *Signs*, Vol. 5, No. 4, 1980

Rosengarten, Frank, *Giacomo Leopardi's Search for a Common Life through Poetry: A Different Nobility, a Different Love*, The Fairleigh Dickinson University Press Series in Italian Studies, 2012

Weisman, Alan, *The World Without Us*, Virgin Books, 2007

The speakers at the climate change conference in section 14 of 'The Great Outdoors' paraphrase sections of Naomi Klein's *This Changes Everything* and Timothy Morton's *Hyperobjects*.

A number of the essays and poems in this volume appeared earlier, in these and in other forms, in literary journals and online.

Many thanks to Jelte, Anne, Arthur, Evi, Hanna, Linde, Olga, Reowin and my parents.

Translator's note

The weather is no longer really just weather, says British philosopher Timothy Morton. It has become an expression of climate.

. . .

The weather was once an everyday phenomenon, a coincidental circumstance that happily did not tend to present itself as a topic of conversation. Today, it has a more defined character. The weather was once a reason to stay home. Today, it's a reason to take to the streets, to protest.
— Ida

Before I read *The Opposite of a Person*, at the end of 2020, the weather's character was, for me, still largely undefined. It was an object (abstract) through which I could express my mood, speaking metaphorically, and one (concrete) that influenced the way I felt, the things I would do on a given day – or, at least, how I would go about doing them. It was light and heat and moisture and wind. It was predictable and unpredictable. It was the weather.

At that time, I was headed for a period of leave from my job as a lecturer, a period in which I was to shift focus from teaching to research, from lesson planning and administering to writing, creating. Right up until the day I applied for it, via a short, two-page form, I didn't believe the research leave would actually happen, it seemed impossible. I told people who asked that it wasn't 'time off' as such, though it might sound that way. When they asked what I would be working on, I informed them that I would be working on a number of projects, but that mainly I would be translating a novel.

From Dutch? they would ask.

Yup, I would say.

What's it about.

It's about climate change – and loneliness. And love. There's an essay in there about homosexuality and coming out, too.

Cool, they would say. That sounds great.

The truth was that I hadn't yet read the novel in full. When I did, I realised that it was in fact a book of hyperobjects,

Timothy Morton's term for those things that are so spatially and temporally vast as to be practically unfathomable.

*

Morton offers global warming as the prime example of a hyperobject; the term, in fact, was picked up by Morton (having been coined by a computer scientist, in 1967, in reference to something far more abstruse) to describe and to attempt to remedy our difficulty, as a species, in recognising the actuality – the existence – of global warming. In Lieke's book, this idea is refracted through the words of a speaker at a climate symposium in Italy. He is 'a friendly-looking middle-aged man' who stands up and says,

> One of the greatest problems with climate change is that it is so elusive. It is everywhere, it will not be isolated, and so no traditional scientific methods can be applied to it. You cannot place 'the climate' under a microscope. Politicians, who have no desire to find solutions to the problem, like to make good use of this. It is of great benefit to them that this phenomenon remains opaque. Complexity makes for intangibility . . . As long as a problem is complex or vague, it is difficult to identify the culprits. There is no point in speaking about 'the climate', because – well, what exactly are we talking about?

In the nineties, he continues, the focal point for global warming – and a relatively effective one – was the ozone layer. For most of us, this was a new term which became a kind of metonym – or synonym, even – for the negative transformation of the Earth's atmosphere. But the unease around the ozone layer faded over time, and so, too, did the sharpness of our collective concern.

In this way, Lieke's work is instrumental: it has goals. What it wants is to draw our attention to the weather, to define its character. To expose the bureaucracy that stands in the way of our tackling the heating up of this planet ('no one would put themselves forward as the first or only national government to commit to the huge expenses that inevitably come along with the attempt to heal the environment') and the hypocrisy of our attempts not to alter our own, human behaviours, but rather the behaviour of the environment itself, via geoengineering – by, for example, dispersing artificial volcanic ash into the air in order to block out the sun's rays. ('Other options currently under research [include] painting the deserts white. I repeat: painting the deserts white.') As the friendly-looking middle-aged man points out, this sort of strategy, rather than offering us an adequate solution, is in fact 'just another expression of the human arrogance that underlies' the problem at the heart of the climate crisis.

*Then an airborne branch strikes Ida's head and at last she
loses, you could say, her consciousness.*

The strength of Lieke's work lies, for me, in its innate, self-acknowledged cognitive dissonance. Her prose is tender-hearted, showing the protagonist Ida and those around her at their most flawed and vulnerable; just as sentimentality is presented as a human weakness, one that might lead us to act, collectively and individually, in ways that turn out to be harmful, it is also what allows us to love Ida, and Ida to love others.

Being a woman, being queer and (arguably) neurologically atypical puts Ida in a difficult position, especially once she falls hopelessly for Robin. Love – any kind of strong emotion, really – is thus figured here as a hyperobject, too, something too diffuse and enormous to condense or express.

The above sentence, in italics, occurs towards the end of the novel, and it is perhaps my favourite in the book. It captures something of that cognitive dissonance, via the qualifier 'you could say', and it also gestures to another of the book's key concerns: the limits of language.

That verbal expression determines the parameters of reality, and that it is simultaneously inadequate, an approximation of something that can never fully be captured in words, are fundamental ideas in the fabric of Ida's worldview.

They're ideas that I've thought a lot about before, and which I've perhaps seen expressed most lucidly by the philosopher and poet Denise Riley. In her book-length essay *Time Lived, Without Its Flow*, Riley tells her readers of her grief for her deceased son and of her resistance to the affect's dominant metaphor, 'time stopped'. She dubs this a 'weak metaphor', one which would 'sap the force from a description of this new state' – not, in this instance, because it doesn't at all correspond to her own experience (the book and its structure are founded on the author's report of a sense 'of being pulled right outside of time' – an experience described by Robin, in *The Opposite of a Person*, as an interminable state of waiting), but rather due to the ubiquity of the expression, its readiness, its seeming accuracy, even. All of which make for a lack of specificity on the part of the individual who picks it up and wields it, given that it offers them no real reason to delve any further into the particularities of their own emotional state. 'Time stopped' works fine, expressing what needs to be expressed, but it also short-circuits what might have become an extended thought, a more detailed thought, and, for that, a stranger, more idiosyncratic and revealing one.

Ida: 'Feelings are formless, so you can't expect to be able to trace their edges with words. Whoever attempts this will be swallowed up by cliché, by any number of one-size-fits-all expressions that in reality describe no one and nothing.'

*

The Opposite of a Person is ultimately a live effort to harness its various hyperobjects through language, to make climate change and love, hopelessness and fear, a reality for its readers. Like Riley, Lieke believes that one way – perhaps the only way – of recording the transitory and conveying the seemingly intangible is through poetry. The presence of poems in this book supports Riley's assertion that '[a] poem may well be carried by oscillation, a to-and-fro, rather than by some forward-leaning chronological drive', that it 'both sanctions and enacts an experience of time which is non-linear'. It is also a means of opening up the reading experience, of allowing room for the reader, of making the text a 'writerly' one (to borrow Roland Barthes' term) in whose authorship the reader must participate. From a recent interview with Lieke, conducted by writer and translator Sarah Timmer Harvey for *Asymptote*:

> If it were possible, readers would always understand exactly what writers are trying to say. But there is a lot of room for interpretation, which is precisely what makes literature so interesting. Yet, it is also proof of the fact that no definition is absolute. Articulating feelings in exactly the right way is something I primarily attempt to do in my poetry, and on rare occasions, I'm able to do it. Then it feels as though I've produced the ultimate characterisation of something and that there'll never be another way to write a feeling or

experience. But then, along comes a reader who manages to turn it into something different after all.

*

That language is fundamentally anthropocentric, human-oriented, should be obvious. That it prioritises consciousness to the degree that it does might come as somewhat of a surprise. Recently, as I was having my hair cut, the apprentice hairdresser was telling me about her linguistics degree. As she massaged shampoo and then conditioner into my hair and scalp, she spoke about syntax, about grammatical subjects and objects, about why we say 'The man stood on the mountain' as opposed to 'The mountain was under the man'.

In the language that currently surrounds translation, the translator is the mountain. As the supposedly subordinate party in the translation dynamic between author, translator and reader, the translator is figured in the language of invisibility and submission (think of the dominant idioms, of the description of the translation as a pane of glass – if you notice its presence, goes the popular wisdom, it's because it contains scratches, pockmarks, fingerprints: imperfections). Here I want to be clear: I view translation as a mode of writing, the translator as co-creator of the text, and the translation process itself as an act of intimacy, not of fidelity.

*

The following quote by poet and translator Don Mee Choi is important to me and to the way I choose to represent myself in the relatively confined space of the Translator's Note:

> For me, contextualising the work may be the most important part of my translation process. All of my nitty-gritty translation decisions, conscious or unconscious, are affected by it. But I won't go into detail about why this word and not that word because details are suffocating to me.

For Choi, the detail is suffocating, a sprawling hyperobject whose definition seems futile, unfeasible. The translated text is a living thing, a creative project which cannot objectively be deemed 'good' or 'bad'. Choi again:

> No, I'm not an agitator. It turns out that I'm a mere imitator, the lowly kind, which is none other than a translator a mimicker of mimetic words in particular. Doubled consonants or certain parts of speech that are repeated on certain occasions, which can be said to be nobody's business, but they are since everything in English is everybody's business. *Farfar swiftswift zealzeal stuffstuff waddlewaddling stickysticky cacklecackled draindrained flowflow yellyell swishswish.* I've just been instructed to get rid of them by an evaluator: Why double up? No, I'm not a collaborator.

What you are reading is a composite voice. It is my rendering of a Dutch voice communicating a story in English to a (most likely) monolingual English speaker, or perhaps a small group of monolingual English speakers. The voice can speak very good English, while English remains her second language. And so, at times, it sounds entirely fluent, while at others it lapses into syntactical patterns that sound closer to those of Dutch. It uses English words that it has read in Morton and in Naomi Klein, in philosophical texts and papers on climate science, in newspapers and on TV, in the poems of Robert Creeley, the lyrics of Joni Mitchell. Its vocabulary is at once surprisingly broad and specific; at other times, it's more limited. Nominally, it is Ida's voice. But the voice of the book is a combination of Lieke and of myself; you will see my fingerprints throughout. This makes it, I hope, a recognisably personal voice. To be entirely smooth and free of so-called imperfections – which are where voice and character are located – would make it something more like the opposite of that.

Sophie Collins
Glasgow & London, 2021